HAPPINESS
AND
SURVIVAL

Also by Bob Gebelein:

Uncle Bobby's Record

Re-Educating Myself:
An Introduction to a New Civilization

The Mental Environment:
(Mostly about Mind Pollution)

Dirty Science:
How Unscientific Methods Are
Blocking Our Cultural Advancement

HAPPINESS
AND
SURVIVAL

BOB GEBELEIN

Published by Robert S. Gebelein
Durham, North Carolina

Contact:
    Robert S. Gebelein
    18 Hawthorne Drive
    Durham, NC 27712
    Email: happinessandsurvival@gmail.com

ISBN 13 PAPER	978-0-9614611-8-8
ISBN 10 PAPER	0-9614611-8-7
ISBN 13 EBOOK	978-0-9614611-9-5
ISBN 10 EBOOK	0-9614611-9-5

Library of Congress Control Number: 2023912594

Manufactured in the United States of America.

To Julia – trying to make the world a better place for you.

Table of Contents

Preface   xi

1. A Fragmented Culture   1
   EGO IS FOREVER   1
   SPIRITUALITY   3
   PHYSICALISM   10
   AUTHORITY   13
   PSYCHOTHERAPY   19
   MY ULTIMATE PHILOSOPHY   26

2. Re-Educating Myself   33
   THE BOMB   33
   THE AMERICAN DREAM COMES TRUE   33
   "THE WASTE LAND"   34
   TURNING MY BACK ON THE CULTURE   35
   WHILE I WAS IN THE ARMY   40
   MY PSYCHOTHERAPY   43
   THE SOCIAL LAWS   53
   WITHDRAWAL   55
   CARL JUNG   56
   DREAM ANALYSIS   58
   BEYOND PSYCHOLOGY   71

3. My Second Journey of Exploration   85

4. The Closing of the American Mind   109
   DISMISSING MESMERISM   111
   DUMPING THE SPIRITUAL   112
   ABANDONING THE STUDY OF THE MIND   115
   GETTING RID OF FREUD   120
   BLOCKING THE ROAD TO SURVIVAL   122

5. What Is Philosophy?   127

6. My Philosophy   135
        MY VISION OF GOVERNMENT   147

7. Forces of Evil (FOE)   151

Quiz   157

List of Dreams

The final exam   *xi*

Everybody does drugs   *4*

My grandmother's death   *41*

SON KICKS FATHER   *44*

Psychologically 10 years old   *58*

Can't make it with a woman   *59*

Sex and Superman   *59*

Naked woman and boys   *61*

The white wolf   *62*

Great ship, 5/7 masts intact   *63*

Lion in the dark   *63*

Light through a fog bank   *64*

Suffering of the lower classes   *65*

My first day in the Coast Guard / The moose principle   *65*

Movie camera car   *71*

Car won't start   *72*

Woman with black lips   75

Dead people coming into my dreams   76

Marijuana is poison   76

Spiritual teacher / Toad one hop from his hole   77

Death experience, up into the presence of the Light   78

Sailboat race, race committee   81

Spooky dreams   83

Editor held me in an iron grip and dragged me down to hell   87

GERALD FORD CARTER   100

Preface

Dream: *It is the final exam. The professor is standing in the front of the room. We are waiting for him to announce the exam question. He announces, "There is no question. You have three hours."*

I am looking for paper to write on, but every piece of paper I find is totally covered by printing. I go out of the building looking for a blank piece of paper, but find none. Finally, I end up in some suburbia with children playing. I realize that I no longer know the way back to the exam room.

Interpretation: People's minds are already thoroughly imprinted with all the things they have learned. There is no way that I am going to get another word in edgewise.

It took me 30 pages to say two simple things in the first chapter, and a year and a half to keep that down to the bare minimum to say these two things, because I had to get around all the opposing beliefs of "A Fragmented Culture."

The first simple thing I say is that every individual is the highest authority to decide for himself or herself what to believe. This is considered "arrogant." We have all received the cultural message, in our authoritarian upbringing, that we must believe persons of status, who are the highest so-called "authorities."

This book is not "authoritative" in that sense, and I am not setting myself up as an "authority." I am just a guy, sharing his knowledge with you. Yes, it is very authoritative, in the sense that it is a better system than your culture has to offer and it works for me in real life. But I am not asking you to accept it on my "authority." I am asking you only to treat the things I am saying as working hypotheses, to be tested by you and verified or not in your own life's experience, on your own authority to decide for yourself what to believe.

The other simple thing is that, because this book has so much to do with psychotherapy, you need to have had some psychotherapy, with positive results, to be able to understand what I am saying in this book. Here, the culture has done a number on psychotherapy. The Hippies rejected it, the academic establishment degraded the kind of people who need it, and the combined psychological defenses of an entire culture got rid of Freud. I don't see how anybody can understand the subtlety and power of psychological defenses without having recognized to some degree, through psychotherapy, one's own psychological defenses.

I will be explaining all this in more detail in Chapter 1.

There seems to be an obsession with editing these days. Even the editor of my latest Harvard reunion report, who had never before changed a word I wrote, had to change my book title *Re-Educating Myself* to *Re-educating Myself*. I suppose they would have to correct T.S. Eliot's poem title "The Waste Land" to "The Wasteland." And I suppose I would cause my publisher some kind of embarrassment if I refused to submit to this kind of obsessive editing.

So I declare that this book is "philosophy," as I define it (not as academic people define it), that philosophy is neither fiction nor nonfiction, but a combination of both, and that therefore the obsessive rules of editing that apply to nonfiction do not apply to this book.

I have my own style of writing which does not conform to *The Chicago Manual of Style*.

I capitalize "Hippies," because they were both a religion and a political party.

I use numbers, as advertising people have taught me to do, where I want to call attention to the numbers, instead of spelling them out.

I use "who" where I should properly use "that," to make it more personal and therefore more interesting, and because I already use "that" too many times.

I capitalize words to emphasize them. Yes, I am shouting.

If my personal style bothers you because of its nonconformities, we can just call it "conversational." I hope that gets around all the rules.

Occasionally I repeat myself. As I explained in my 1970 manuscript, painting has been described as a two-dimensional representation of a three-dimensional object. Similarly, I described writing as a one-dimensional representation of an n-dimensional object. The problem is where to cut the net to make it all come out as one string. And then wherever I have cut, there I have lost a connection and have to repeat something. It is probably easier to tolerate my repetitions than to understand what I am saying here.

I thank the Lord, God, for choosing me, Christ for protecting me, and the angels for helping me write this book.

Bob Gebelein, June 23, 2023

Chapter 1
A Fragmented Culture

EGO IS FOREVER

I was sitting at the yoga retreat enjoying my ayurvedic lunch, but I wasn't enjoying the lecture from the spiritual teacher coming to us over the sound system, telling us we had to get rid of the ego. First of all, he wasn't telling us what he meant by "ego." Was it the ego itself, or ego-compensation, or ego-defenses that we had to get rid of? He wasn't saying. He was just talking as if we knew exactly what he was talking about.

"Ego" is defined in my 1996 *Merriam-Webster's Collegiate Dictionary* simply as "the self." I define it further by saying it is the real self, as contrasted to the artificial self that many people have created, like a character in a movie, because society has pressured them into abandoning their real selves.

I found my real self, who was a small child, and brought him up to maturity, with the help of psychotherapy and dream analysis. I found happiness for myself, and actually spiritual strength, by strengthening the ego, not getting rid of it.

I have here the book, *No Self No Problem*, by Chris Niebauer, Ph.D. It asserts that the idea of a "self" is an illusion. It says that brain scans have never found an area in the physical brain that identifies with the "self."

This assumes that if the "self" doesn't exist within the physical brain, it doesn't exist. This goes along with the assumption, widely held by scientists, that "The mind is nothing but the physical brain." These assumptions are refuted by people who have memories of past lives.

Reincarnation research has discovered that there are small children who have memories of past incarnations. These children remember what their name was in their previous incarnation and where they lived. The researchers go there and find out that there really was such a person. They contact the person's previous family and set up a meeting with the child. When the child meets his or her former family, friends, and enemies, he or she recognizes them and exhibits the appropriate emotions.

This was first publicized in 1966 by Ian Stevenson in *Twenty Cases Suggestive of Reincarnation*. The Division of Perceptual Studies at the University of Virginia has since found more than 2500 cases suggestive of reincarnation.

These studies have been replicated by other researchers, although they have not done as many studies, and they have all worked with Ian Stevenson, so you can say that they are all in cahoots. But the detail of the reports and the scientific tone suggests otherwise. They have also established a 6-step procedure to guard against fraud and other errors.

There exists a belief in the scientific establishment that there is no reality beyond the physical. Not all scientists share this belief, but it is enforced in our accredited academic institutions by what I call "hard ridicule:" Academic people can lose their jobs if they take a serious interest in the spiritual. The only reason that the research on reincarnation at the University of Virginia has been allowed to exist is because it has been supported by a grant from Chester Carlson, the founder of Xerox, specifically for the study of the spiritual.

I define "the scientific establishment" as those scientists, the vast majority of scientists, that study physical phenomena with the physical senses – the physicists, chemists, biologists, astronomers, geologists, and so forth. They have been highly successful. They are established. They have rightfully earned the very highest status in our culture.

Because of their high status, their opinions are taken seriously in areas where they are uninformed, namely the mental and the spiritual, where actually their opinions represent an extreme bias, which they enforce with their "hard ridicule."

In particular, they take the position that any physical explanation is preferable to any spiritual explanation. This creates an infinite bias in favor of the physical. With this way of thinking, nothing spiritual is ever going to be found. This is an error that needs to be corrected.

Also in Western civilization, we have the arbitrary convention called "Occam's Razor," asserting that the simplest explanation is almost always the best. That biases people towards simple solutions.

I am suggesting that we change that. I am suggesting that we accept the most reasonable explanation. I am sure that that is what people did before they had Occam's razor.

Yes, there are all kinds of cockamamie explanations of how these children would know the correct names of dead people and the places where they lived, and how they exhibited appropriate emotions, rivaling the abilities of the best child actors, upon meeting people they allegedly knew in the past. But the most reasonable explanation is that they are genuine. They have reincarnated. They really were that person in the past life.

And to refute it, it is necessary to refute all 2500 cases.

Not only is reincarnation proved here, but also the fact that the mind, or at least the memory, can survive without the physical brain. Near-death experiences don't prove this, because the people always come back to the same physical body with the same physical brain. But in these cases of reincarnation these memories have survived without a physical brain.

So, to go back to the "self" being imaginary because it can't be found in the physical brain, that is because the "I" is independent of the physical brain. The child is aware of "I am" and "I was," and the "I" carries over to inhabit both bodies.

Not only does the "self" exist; it exists forever.

SPIRITUALITY

We have had more than half a century of "spirituality." In the late 1960s, large numbers of young people blasted themselves off into inner space with psychedelic drugs and became Hippies. They opened up their minds artificially to the spiritual. I say "artificially" because psychologically they weren't ready to deal with it. Yes, the insights and the visions they had were real, but their typical American upbringing did not equip them mentally to assimilate the experience into their worldview. It literally "blew their minds."

We have the word "traumatic" to mean an experience that a person is unable to assimilate into his or her worldview, causing a psychological problem. But "traumatic" carries with it the meaning that the experience was unpleasant. I don't know of any word to indicate that a person developed a psychological problem from a pleasant experience.

The psychedelic drug experience was that kind of an experience for most people. It gave them the greatest pleasure – joy and exhilaration. It did not give them pain, fear, or anger, except in the case of a "bad trip." The emotion was more likely one of awe. It was literally an "awesome" experience.

But there was nothing in their American belief structure to enable them to comprehend this extremely pleasant experience. They were psychologically traumatized by it. I have to use an improper word, because I don't know any proper word for it.

Our American culture had nothing to help them deal with this spiritual experience, so they went to India and discovered Eastern philosophy, gurus, meditation, and yoga. Richard Alpert, who became Baba (Saint) Ram Dass, eventually became disillusioned with both psychedelic drugs and meditation. But millions of people read his books because they shared the same psychedelic experience and were looking for answers.

Because there were so many of them, the Hippies became the market for any books on the advancement of the culture. Books that did not conform to their beliefs were simply not published. So the whole culture has been swept along in the Hippie quest for "spirituality."

Most of the people alive on earth today were not yet born in the Summer of Love. So I suspect that most of you have not been traumatized by psychedelic drugs. (The night after I first said that, I had a little dream that told me, "Everybody does drugs.") So, OK, I admit that I don't know who does drugs and who is traumatized by it. But whether or not we have done drugs, we all have a life to live on earth. This book I am writing now is not about "spirituality," but is about how I have dealt with the challenges of living a life here on earth, for personal happiness and survival of the species.

In the mid-1990s, I bought about half a dozen books from the Institute Of Noetic Sciences (IONS). They were all on different subjects, but they all rejected logic, science, ego, and psychotherapy, and they all changed the definitions of the words "truth" and "reality" into one's perception of "truth" and one's perception of "reality." This is all totally different from my view.

Yes, I can understand that people lose logic when they are on an LSD trip and believe "I am the chair." They have to know "I am not the chair" for there to be any point in saying, "I am the chair." I am the chair and not the chair at the same time. Logic is lost, and this is just fine.

But to survive in this physical world, we need logic. Without logic, we would all die immediately in head-on collisions.

I can understand why people reject science: because they fail to differentiate between science and the belief that is held within the scientific community that there is no reality beyond the physical. We can reject that belief and at the same time accept science itself for the contributions it has made to our knowledge of the physical reality.

As for rejecting the ego, I question whether this is even possible. First of all, one has to define what is meant by "ego." I read the first 180 pages of the book *Beyond Ego* that I bought from IONS and never found a definition of "ego."

"Ego" is one's sense of self, including one's self-esteem. People with weak egos and low self-esteem create a grandiose image of themselves to compensate for the pain of the low self-esteem. This is ego-compensation. I compare it to the bloated bellies of starving people. Put some real food in those bellies and the swelling goes down. In the same way, if people could find their real selves and develop them to their true potential as human beings, there would be no need for ego-compensation, and the artificial swelling would go down. I found happiness by strengthening the ego, not getting rid of it.

Ego-defenses are those false beliefs people have to create to support the grandiose false image. Where there is no ego-compensation, there is no need for ego-defenses. I am what I am.

Or maybe what these gurus mean by getting rid of the ego is what I experienced at the psychological age of puberty, when the exclusive self-interest of the child gave way to an equally natural motivation to give and share and even sacrifice myself for others. This compassion and altruism did not come from a loss of ego, but by extending my love for myself to a love for all humanity.

Because these New-Age gurus don't define what they mean by "ego," it is really foolish to argue with them. They could always see "ego" as something else.

I can understand that LSD can take away ego, just as it takes away logic, and in taking away this sense of self, people would have feelings of compassion and altruism. But again, without ego, we would all die immediately in head-on collisions.

As for rejecting psychotherapy, this was done with the slogan, "Psychiatrists are tools of the Establishment." According to Sidney Cohen, MD, in *The Beyond Within*, one of the effects of LSD is to make people more suggestible. Because of this, the Hippies instantly believed slogans such as "You can't trust anybody over 30." This caused them some embarrassment in later life, when they were all over 30. Similarly, in their highly suggestible state, the slogan "Psychiatrists are tools of the Establishment" was instantly believed.

I learned years later from an aging Hippie that this slogan was based on institutional psychiatrists. Well, of course, psychiatrists that were being paid by the Establishment worked to serve the interests of the Establishment. But my psychiatrist, who was paid by me, worked to serve my interests, and actually helped me to break free of the Establishment.

Actually, I first heard the slogan "Psychiatrists are tools of the Establishment" from an academic person in 1960, several years before the Hippies picked it up. The academic establishment has had a major role in rejecting psychotherapy for themselves and degrading people who would benefit by it.

But for me, psychotherapy was the way to my personal happiness, and I see it also as the way to survival of the species.

In the early 1960s, when I was going to a psychiatrist in New York, most of my friends in New York were also in psychotherapy. It was what young people did for personal growth – not just the wife-beaters and the substance-abusers, but the cultural leaders. A 1972 study by Kenneth Howard and David Orlinsky identified "Type One Clients" as mostly young, attractive, relatively affluent, verbal, college-educated, culturally sophisticated, unmarried, and female (*Annual Review of Psychology: XXIII*). These are the kind of people that might be involved in spiritual disciplines today.

Present-day academic people don't believe there were ever such studies or such people to study. Psychotherapy for personal growth has become out of fashion, with the drug revolution leading people into "spirituality" and meditation and yoga. That's a deadly argument, that anything has become out of fashion. All I can say is that our credentialed people in our accredited academic institutions are not supposed to operate on the basis of fashion. I aim to show, in the course of this book, that Freud and Jung and all those others in the field of psychotherapy gave us too much truth about ourselves, and the collective psychological defenses of an entire culture got rid of them.

Actually, in regard to spirituality, I was looking up "psychological defenses" one day on the Internet and came across "spiritual bypassing," a discovery by John Welwood, a Buddhist. He discovered that people can't succeed at spiritual disciplines while they have psychological problems. Those psychological problems work their way in disguise into everything they do.

My conclusion from that is that resolving one's psychological problems is a necessary first step in true spiritual growth. Psychotherapy is spirituality. M. Scott Peck in *The Road Less Traveled* made that point without ever getting beyond the psychotherapy of his day. Carl Jung took us farther into the spiritual, but he was ahead of his time and dismissed as a "mystic."

The other side of "spiritual bypassing" is that it serves as ego-compensation for people with ailing egos. The first thing I noticed about the Hippies was their attitude of "We are spiritual. We are superior." "Spirituality" can take you a long way believing you are superior before you discover that it is just an ego boost.

My path to happiness and survival here on earth includes logic, science, ego, and psychotherapy, four things that were unanimously rejected in the books I received from IONS. I am wondering why, in order to be "spiritual," one has to reject things that are beneficial to life on earth. Or maybe we are just being given wrong information.

Switching the meanings of the words "truth" and "reality" into one's perception of truth and reality has worked its way into academic thinking as "postmodernism" and legitimized thereby, as if it were a new and more accurate way of thinking. It is new, but it is not accurate. I believe its origins were in people's psychedelic drug experience, of discovering things that were previously outside what the culture saw as "reality," and having to coin expressions such as "alternative realities" and "multiple realities" to explain them.

It is all part of one reality, and we know very little of it.

I define "reality" as the collection of everything that exists. There is one and only one reality, just as there is one and only one "everything." Like the blind men and the elephant, we are aware only of that part of it that we can grasp. All of our perceptions of it are different, but there is only one "reality," independent of anybody's perception of it.

There is the New Age slogan, "You create your reality."

I struggled with that one for years: Yes, you create the spin on the ball to satisfy your own psychological needs, but you do not create the ball.

And then after fifty or so years, it dawned on me that the Hippies' definition of "reality" made it a true statement. If "your reality" is defined as your perception of reality, then of course you create it.

But the statement, in its ambiguity, creates confusion, and confusion can lead to insanity.

I define "truth" as an accurate representation or description of the reality or that portion of the reality which it represents. Actually, I avoid the word "truth" because it has been so distorted or misrepresented, as in "*Pravda*" means "Truth."

Truth is simply the quality of accuracy. It doesn't have to be absolute truth, as in absolute accuracy. There are degrees of accuracy, which can be thought of as the number of decimal places of accuracy. Professional philosophers have argued that we don't see the cells and the atoms and the sub-atomic particles, and therefore we don't see the absolute reality. That is true. But at least we can have the best perception of the reality that our senses will give us.

The Hippie meaning of "truth," one's perception of truth, has nothing to do with quality or accuracy. There is something beyond "my truth" and "my reality." I approach an understanding of reality with better and better approximations, with the kind of respect for ultimate truth that a mathematician has when approaching infinity. The better I understand this reality, the more likely it is that my life will lead to happiness and survival than to somewhere else.

Again, I can be confronted with the deadly argument that my thinking is out of date because it isn't postmodernism.

The mental, in "spirituality," is thought of as a source of error. But we all have minds, and our minds decide what to do in this lifetime. If our own minds aren't making that decision, somebody else's is doing that for us. The mind that is telling us that our mind is a source of error could be a source of error. The mind is a part of what we are as human beings, and the people who are telling us to get rid of it are asking us to do the impossible – maybe possible in meditating but not in tying a shoelace.

In the same way, the guru that is telling us to get rid of fear and anger is asking us to do the impossible. This is part of what we are when we are incarnated into physical bodies. The best we can do is to try to channel these drives in constructive ways.

The Hippies were spiritual. They were superior. They did have many good insights. I have no doubt that what they saw on their LSD trips was the truth, and a higher level of awareness than most of us are conscious of in this earthly existence. But then they had to come back down into the earthly personalities they were without the drugs, with minds blown from the experience. And in that not-so-superior state, the feeling of superiority became ego-compensation. And in their psychological need to defend that feeling of superiority, they became very good at putting other people down.

What did the Hippies actually do? They stole things from me. They stole my best sweater and my favorite T-shirts. They stole my Simon & Garfunkel records and replaced them with Kingston Trio records. That's what I called a "Hippie trade." You take something you want and replace it with something you don't want. What's wrong with that?

Hippies broke the law and then turned around and made it look like the law was at fault, by calling the police officer "Pig." They burned down the ROTC building at Kent State and kept the firefighters from getting near it. But all we know about Kent State was that the National Guard killed 4 peaceful protesters. There were hundreds or thousands of instances of the Hippies seriously breaking the law, but the Hippies were always able to make it seem that they were the righteous ones and the law was at fault. They would hassle you and then turn around and say, "You wouldn't hassle me, would you?"

They advanced the art of mental warfare well beyond Joe McCarthy's level, in a society that still doesn't know what mental warfare is. They could destroy you with a single word. Nobody dared argue with them. And so they swept the whole culture along with them in this thing they called "spirituality."

Is this "spirituality," or is this forces of evil (FOE) at work?

The Hippies, in all their teachings, never acknowledge the presence of evil in the spiritual environment. But it is reasonable to assume, if there is evil here on earth – destructive forces – that there is evil in the spiritual domain. Hitler and Saddam Hussein have not ceased to exist, just because their physical bodies are dead. Are the Hippies being naive in not recognizing evil in the spiritual? And how much of this evil have they unknowingly brought into our culture in the name of "spirituality?" I might conclude, when I see that many of these teachings are wrong, that this is a deliberate effort to mislead us. In any event, "spirituality" is not giving us the right answers for happiness and survival in this earth environment.

PHYSICALISM

"Physicalism" is the belief that there is no reality beyond the physical. The scientific establishment and the whole academic subculture are dominated by it. Anybody who has ever been to college has been exposed to it, and many people have been indoctrinated into it.

I believe it all started when the Theory of Evolution replaced the Biblical account of how life on earth was created.

Charles Darwin observed that living creatures adjust to their environment by a process of random mutation and natural selection. Those changes which enable individuals to survive and produce more offspring than other members of their species will eventually become the predominant characteristics of the species. This process is called "adaptation."

Darwin theorized from this that new species evolved from other species by this same process of random mutation and natural selection.

It didn't take long for others to extend his theory and say that life itself had evolved out of the primeval muck by chance combination of chemicals.

With this purely physical explanation of how life and all living creatures evolved, there was no need for a Creator to explain their existence. God and the whole spiritual realm were simply rejected in favor of this new scientific explanation.

This became the dominant belief in the academic community, and after being held for a century and a half, it is now held with such absolute certainty by the physicalists that anybody who believes there is such a thing as the spiritual is treated as if he or she was mentally deficient.

There have been hints over the years that we operate in more dimensions than just the physical, by the British Society for Psychical Research, Mary Baker Eddy, William James, Edgar Cayce, Rudolf Steiner, Carl Jung, J.B. Rhine, Ian Stevenson, Richard Kieninger, the Hippies, and many others. In response to this accumulating evidence, the physicalists, in their absolute certainty, say, "The spiritual does not exist; therefore the evidence must be flawed."

Yes, there is a mountain of evidence supporting evolution. And there is a mountain of evidence showing how species adapt to their environment through a process of random mutation and natural selection. But is there evidence to show that new species, and even life itself, were created by this process of adaptation?

I read in the 1983 *Encyclopedia Britannica* that a new species had appeared much more quickly in geological time than could be explained by the slow process of adaptation. This was explained away with the theory of "punctuated equilibria," which said that some catastrophic change to the environment had forced the species to evolve quickly. But then to prove this, one would have to show the catastrophic change to the environment for each species that appeared more quickly than expected by adaptation. A biologist I talked to said that the most likely outcome of a catastrophic change to the environment would be extinction.

Many years later I read about the Cambrian Explosion, where many new species appeared fully formed, with no evidence of any gradual transition from previously existing species.

I credit Richard Milton, in *Shattering the Myths of Darwinism*, for giving me the best evidence that adaptation cannot create new species: Plant and animal breeders over the years have observed that there are natural boundaries to the changes that can be made to a species. Ernst Mayr called it "genetic homeostasis" (Milton, page 135). There is a norm for every species where individuals are more robust than those at the fringes. Those individuals at the fringes tend to become sterile. Thus the mathematics of natural selection favors those closer to the norm. Without concentrated efforts of selected breeding (or other such hereditary pressures), all offspring would eventually revert to the norm. So if there are these forces keeping members of a species from going to its fringes, it is even less likely that they would be able to cross over and become another species. Some other kind of a force has to be at work.

If the best efforts of human beings are unable to create a new species, random mutation is not likely to do it. And if the best efforts of human beings are unable to create a new species, that does suggest that a higher intelligence is necessary.

Richard Kieninger learned from the Brotherhoods that angels created new species by genetic engineering when the environment was ready to support those species. I present this here only as a hypothesis. It fits the evidence better than Darwin's theory, taking into account the chronology of evolution (as opposed to the Biblical account that God created everything in 6 days in 4004 BC).

But when I presented this explanation in my review on Amazon of *Why Evolution Is True*, by Jerry Coyne, it was met with total ridicule. (Sorry – they took away the long string of ridicule. There was one person who said I was "hilarious" about 50 times, like a drive-by shooting.)

If we are not allowed even to hypothesize – to ask the question – what does this do to science? Doesn't this create a huge bias which blocks scientific inquiry, all in the name of "science?" I was only being ridiculed, but academic people can lose their reputations, their academic careers, and their whole social existence, just by asking the question.

All academic people know that ridicule is not a legitimate argument.

But establishment scientists have forced this belief in a purely physical reality on the academic community with unscientific arguments such as authoritarian pronouncements, ridicule, and power politics. Because they have credentials, they are believed. Having credentials should mean that they are right, but actually having credentials (from the Latin *"credo,"* meaning "I believe") means they can say anything they want and be believed.

I have been advised not to bring truth to power. But these people don't think of themselves as representing power. They think of themselves as representing truth. Harvard's motto is *"Veritas,"* not

"*Auctoritas.*" But it is because of their credentials that people are listening to them. Their credentials represent power, and give them the power to disregard the truth. When they make the authoritarian pronouncement "The spiritual does not exist," they think it is the truth, but to me it is evidence that they know absolutely nothing about the spiritual.

From this position of power, they can ridicule people. Ridicule is an invalid argument. It is just verbal assault. But for academic people who take a serious interest in nonphysical phenomena, this ridicule can cause them to be treated as if they are mentally incompetent, shunned by their colleagues, and denied publication, funding, and employment. That is why I call it "hard ridicule."

Not all academic people hold to this quasi-religious belief, only the ones I call "physicalists," but the others are intimidated by the ridicule, which is truly powerful and can cause them to lose their academic careers. So it is hard to tell which ones are the physicalists and which ones are only being silenced by the ridicule. If they go with the ridicule they are not doing their jobs, but if they oppose it, they can lose their jobs.

With these kinds of pressures from the methods of power, the academic establishment can hardly be expected to represent "truth," as much as they think they are dedicated to it.

This view of a purely physical reality poses as "science." But it is not science. It is prejudice, based on ignorance. The Hippies exposed that with their first-hand view of the spiritual.

I feel that both views were necessary for the advancement of our culture. Physicalism was necessary in order to break away from the authoritarianism of organized religion, and spirituality was necessary to break away from the authoritarianism of physicalism. But both groups, the physicalists and the Hippies, have their own obsessions that we need to get away from. I am going to show you how to break free of authoritarianism and recognize your own authority.

AUTHORITY

Who am I to be saying that respected spiritual teachers are wrong? Who am I to say I know better than credentialed academic people?

The first step I took, in my quest for happiness and survival, was to make my own mind the highest authority to decide for myself what to believe. This was so radically different from our accepted cultural beliefs that I was called "arrogant" when I first said it. Surely I wasn't the greatest mind or the most knowledgeable person. But my own mind has to decide what to believe, whether I am knowledgeable or not. The only thing arrogant about it was that I did not make it so. My own mind has always been the highest authority to decide for myself what to believe. This is true for everybody. Our own minds are the highest authority to decide for ourselves what to believe, right from the beginning.

But as children, we delegate that authority to our elders. Most of us come into this world knowing nothing consciously. Some of us remember past incarnations, and others remember existing in a spiritual realm, but for all of us our physical brains have been newly created, and they need to be programmed. We need software for living. We need knowledge of the world we live in and rules of behavior in that world. These things are supplied in an authoritarian way by parents and teachers and preachers.

When we are small children, our parents are like gods to us, all-powerful and all-knowing. We are happy to believe whatever they want to teach us, upon their "authority" as gods. In school we learn that whatever our teachers teach us is "knowledge," on the "authority" of the teacher, and our job is only to memorize it. In Sunday school we learn that the teachings come from the very highest "authority," the "authority" of God.

I put the word "authority" in quotes here to indicate that it is "so-called 'authority.'" The real authority is our authority to decide for ourselves what to believe, as opposed to this so-called "authority" of persons of status.

First of all, how do we even know that they are right, if their knowledge reaches far beyond our own? There is a very high probability that they are right, but how would we know if they weren't? We would need a level of knowledge equal to or greater than theirs. Most people accept the high probability that the "authorities" are correct.

We are thus conditioned in our childhood to believe things on other people's "authority." We develop "authority hooks." That is, when another person speaks in an authoritative voice or gives us a command, we believe or obey accordingly. We are not only conditioned intellectually; we are also conditioned emotionally.

This conditioning on the basis of other people's so-called "authority" I call our "authoritarian" upbringing. Belief on the basis of somebody else's "authority" I call "authoritarianism."

I am using the words "authoritarian" and "authoritarianism" here only in terms of belief and not in terms of power. But my dictionary (Merriam-Webster, 1996) defines these words only in terms of power, synonymous with "totalitarian" and "totalitarianism." So it seems that belief on the basis of somebody else's supposed "authority" is so ingrained in our culture that it is invisible – there is no word for it. It is like the saying that if fish had a language they would have no word for "water."

Our authoritarian upbringing is so engrained and so invisible that one critic said that my book title *Re-Educating Myself* was "circular." In other words, this person could not imagine education without an external teacher in the role of "authority."

Some people take advantage of this childhood conditioning to set themselves up as "authorities." They don't really know what they are talking about, but then they know that you don't have the expert knowledge to dispute them. They just push all the buttons of your childhood conditioning and you become a willing disciple. The "self-help" books I have seen fall into this category. They aren't really self-help at all, but somebody else telling you what to do with your life and counting on the fact that you are so conditioned that you don't know the difference.

The prime example of people setting themselves up as "authorities" is religion. Religion does many good things in the world. We all know that. But religion does bad things, too. Religion deals largely with the unknown. Religion is mainly fiction when it attempts to explain the unknown. Based on a few true glimpses of the spiritual, it claims to know the absolute and ultimate truth. Religion pretends to know what it does not know. This is misinformation. This is bad.

If all religions and all cosmologies shared precisely the same absolute and ultimate truth, that would indicate that they are all true. But they are all different. That means that at most only one is truly the absolute and ultimate truth. And if that one happens to be the one you believe in, that makes it suspect. The most likely truth is that none of them are the absolute and ultimate truth they claim to be.

But to maintain their "authority," they have to stick with this claim of absolute and ultimate truth, "God's own Truth," as the first principle of their thinking, and therefore any deviation has to come from evil forces. This of course leads to religious persecutions, wars, and genocide.

So the first step for sanity in the world would be for all religions to concede that they don't have the absolute and ultimate truth, and to share the spiritual insights that they do have with each other and with all of humanity.

Religion carries this childhood conditioning to believe in "authorities" all the way through adulthood. If all the priesthood were to die off or mysteriously disappear, we would have to create other "authorities" to take their place, because there is a social need for it. (This actually happened when scientists rejected religion. Then scientists became the priesthood that is now believed on their "authority.")

From the time we are small children and see our parents as gods, the image of the idealized parental authority figure (IPAF) is imprinted in our minds. The IPAF has to be perfect, hence "idealized." If an IPAF makes a mistake, it can be traumatic for a child and a cause for extreme anger throughout one's life. We get rid of the IPAF by recognizing that our parents and all "authority" figures are human beings and make mistakes, just like everybody else.

As children grow up, they begin to see that the grownups aren't always right – that they are not as gods, all-knowing and all-powerful. The children share this knowledge, developing what I call "a juvenile rebellion against adult authority (JRAAA)." Leaders among children push this button. Your parents want you to be "good," so in order to gain the approval of your peers, you have to be "bad."

As children become teenagers, there is a very natural and well-known rebellion against adult authority. I am not saying that the child is usually right. A great source of annoyance to me as a teenager was that my father was usually right. But the child is exercising that authority to decide for himself or herself what is right and wrong.

It is a natural thing that teenagers question and rebel against adult authority, because as our minds develop to almost an adult level, we are able to see more and more the flaws in "the system."

And it should be equally natural, as we reach adulthood, that we break free of seeing other adults as "authorities" and recognize that we ourselves are the highest authorities to decide for ourselves what to believe.

We are told that to be adults, we are supposed to be responsible. But responsibility means admitting you have the authority. You can't have responsibility without authority.

The child is wise to delegate that authority to adults who obviously know more than he or she does. But when the child becomes an adult, he or she is equal to other adults.

Well, not really. There are a great many people who are knowledgeable in a great many areas. There are experts in many fields – plumbers, electricians, doctors, lawyers. One does not really know how expert they are unless one is expert oneself.

I have a book on Indian philosophy that tells me about things that "the seers" know. This is not only far beyond what I know, but it is also far beyond what I am capable of knowing, with my particular abilities. So do I just have to believe what they are saying? No, I don't, because in my ignorance I don't know for certain they are right.

The acceptance of one's own ultimate authority to decide what to believe I identify as the coming of age into adulthood.

My personal coming of age was on the day before the start of classes at Harvard in 1952. They packed our entire freshman class of 1200 into Sanders Theatre and gave us official permission to think for ourselves, to use our own minds. This was a radical step after an authoritarian upbringing. It gave me a great sense of freedom, as if my mind was being released from prison. It seemed foolish to disagree with professors who were experts in their fields, but at least it put the idea in our heads.

I give credit to Harvard for performing this ceremony at an appropriate time in our lives and helping us to recognize what had always been true – that our own minds were the highest authority to decide what to believe.

The people who don't believe in global warming are exercising this authority, even though I personally think they are wrong. Yes, they are right in not believing scientists just because scientists have status. But they can look at the evidence for themselves. They can look at pictures of glaciers in 1950, compared to now. Or if they think that pictures in a book are faked, they can look at the real evidence, as I did.

In 1951, we were catching tuna in Cape Cod Bay, and people were catching bluefish off of Montauk Point, Long Island. By 1985, there were 180 boats in Cape Cod Bay catching bluefish, and the tuna had moved north to Nova Scotia. The fish know more about global warming than some people.

I am not writing here as an "authority." Yes, I am absolutely certain of everything I am saying here. If I am not certain, I will hedge. But I don't expect you to believe any of it on my so-called "authority." You, the reader, have the ultimate authority, first to decide whether you want to read this, and then to decide whether you want to believe any of it.

Can I call this "self-help?" Actually, "self-help" is a psychological defense for people who don't want to go to a legitimate licensed psychotherapist. "Self-help" books are usually written by people who are setting themselves up as "authorities" and telling you how to run your life. That's not really "self-help." These "authorities" are taking advantage of the "authority hooks" we all have from our authoritarian upbringing. We respond obediently to anybody speaking with authority. True self-help is breaking free from that kind of "authority" and acting on your own judgment.

This is my approach to self-help. I am writing about how I helped myself, and I am offering my experience as an example of how you might help yourself. I am not ordering you to do anything. You can simply decide whether my experience applies to you or not.

I use the pronoun "I" to describe my experience because it is more accurate than saying "you" or "we" and pretending that my experience applies to more people than myself. It is up to you, on your own authority, to decide whether my experience applies to you.

I am asking you, the reader, not to believe anything I say on my "authority," but to accept the things I say only as working hypotheses, to be tested in your own life's experience.

I am following here the lead of the Brotherhoods, as described by Richard Kieninger. The Brotherhoods (both male and female) are some of the most highly developed and knowledgeable people on this planet. They teach that their teachings are not to be taken as Gospel truth, but only as working hypotheses, to be tested in one's life-experience. What is good enough for the Brotherhoods is certainly good enough for me.

The Brotherhoods also teach the difference between "information" and "knowledge." What is read in a book is only "information." (And it could be misinformation or disinformation.) It does not become "knowledge" until you have tested it in your life's experience and found it to be true.

This means that everything you ever learned from your parents, your teachers, religious leaders, gurus, and all the books you ever read, including the Bible, are only information to be tested and verified in your own experience before it becomes "knowledge." What I am saying here, too, is only "information." You are the authority.

PSYCHOTHERAPY

My way to happiness, and the way that I discovered for survival of the species, has been through psychotherapy – not psychotherapy as it might be known to you or as it might be practiced by professionals, because I don't know exactly what that is, but psychotherapy as I experienced it. When I use the word "psychotherapy," it should be understood that I am talking about psychotherapy as I experienced it, and not necessarily psychotherapy as another person might know it or might have been led to believe. So you will have to pay attention to what I am saying, just to know what I am talking about when I say "psychotherapy." To begin with, my idea of psychological maturity goes well beyond normal.

People have complained that I am "advertising" psychotherapy, putting that sleazy connotation on what I am doing. I am not advertising psychotherapy. I am not in a position to be making money from it. I am only a satisfied customer. This is my testimonial that Freud's methods work. Again, nobody is paying me for this.

Some bad things have been said about psychotherapy and about Freud, who invented it. To start with, there has always been a stigma attached to undergoing psychotherapy, from the days when crazy people were thought to be possessed by the Devil. First of all, psychotherapy as I experienced it doesn't work with crazy people, as I have said, but with people with relatively mild mental disorders. Freud's book title was not "The Psychopathology of Crazy People" but was *The Psychopathology of Everyday Life*, suggesting that most of us in the normal range have psychological problems.

The psychological profession tried to tell us that having psychological problems was not a moral offense, but was like being sick – not our fault. But still the stigma was attached to undergoing psychotherapy. My psychiatrist warned me in 1959 not to tell my employer that I was in therapy. I had trouble in 1968 getting a security clearance when I admitted that I had gone to a psychiatrist. The thinking on their part was "Once stigmatized, always stigmatized." There was no provision in the stigma for actually having resolved one's psychological problems. This stigma against psychotherapy is on the same level as religious and racial prejudice. Actually, the stigma is a psychological defense by those who want to believe they don't need therapy because they are superior to those who need it.

And then, in 2014, I saw that the stigma had sunk to a whole new level. An academic person started to snicker when I said I had been through psychotherapy, and then stopped abruptly when he saw that I was serious. (A person that is psychologically mature can stop these people in their tracks just by staring them down.) I was a person that that person had been conditioned by his peers to ridicule. The kind of people who went through psychotherapy had been degraded and demeaned by the academic community. We weren't of their kind. We were an inferior kind of people, like wife-beaters and substance-abusers. Certainly nobody with academic credentials needed psychotherapy. It was beneath them. And certainly anybody with academic credentials known to be going through psychotherapy would have been ridiculed by his or her peers and shunned socially.

I just happened to come across the story of how physicist Wolfgang Pauli consulted with Carl Jung, and how he feared there would be a "hellish laughter" if his fellow elite physicists ever found out.

But hellish laughter, ridicule, social snobbery, peer-group pressure, and social ostracism are not legitimate arguments. Every academic person knows that. So why are they bound by these illegitimate arguments? To understand that, you need to know what psychological defenses are. And to understand that, you need to know what psychotherapy is.

Psychotherapy as I experienced it is an education, a different kind of education from the intellectual education we are all familiar with. It is a development of our mental potential, from the childhood level where most of us are stuck, to something more nearly approaching our adult potential. It is more akin to weight-lifting (no pain, no gain) than to book learning. It is a growth process, like learning to play a sport or a musical instrument. It is not enough just to memorize the process; you have to do it.

Psychotherapy as I experienced it represents a whole new way of thinking. It began with Freud, was improved upon by Jung, and was further improved upon by many others, including myself. But when I am telling you about the discoveries of Freud and Jung, it is not just because I have read about these things in a book. It is because I have verified these things in my own experience.

Freud discovered that people didn't always do what they consciously intended to do. In my case, I seemed to fail sometimes when I consciously wanted to succeed. Freud deduced from that that there was a subconscious component as well as a conscious component of people's minds that determined how people actually lived their lives.

Freud discovered that morality didn't work; it only drove our real desires into the subconscious, from whence they acted out in disguised ways.

Buried in that subconscious was a real self with real emotions that were more powerful than the conscious intellect. These emotions could bend, warp, and twist the conscious intellect into supporting anything they wanted it to believe, by a process known as "rationalization." A "rationalization," by my definition, is an argument that is not quite accurate, but is accurate enough to be believed by somebody who really wants to believe it.

And so the wisdom of the twentieth century became "We believe what we want to believe." And to compensate for that, people tried to bend the other way, to focus on dingy cities and unrewarding lives and certainly no loving God to save us from all that. Of course the negative is just as much a distortion of the truth as the positive. What we want is for our thinking to be accurate, and psychotherapy does that for us, by bringing the subconscious material into consciousness, where it is no longer distorting us with ulterior motives.

Our lessons in school are geared to our abilities as children, but our lessons in life are not. Children are traumatized by events involving pain, fear, or anger that their philosophy is not developed enough to comprehend. Their minds store the memory of the experience, parts or all of which become subconscious. Then the subconscious acts in a disguised way to put the person into situations, and to draw the person into situations, similar to the one that caused the trauma, over and over again, until it is finally resolved, if ever. The Hippies called this a "hang-up."

We grow physically automatically. As our body grows, our brain grows, and our intelligence grows with it. As our intelligence grows and our experience grows with it, we become better able to behave appropriately and deal philosophically with life's problems. This is what I call "psychological growth" or "psychological development."

But psychological growth is not automatic, as is physical growth. Psychological growth can be "arrested," as Freud discovered, by a traumatic experience, leaving the person at the same behavioral and philosophical level they had when they had the traumatic experience. This is part of the mind's strategy to recreate the same situation over and over again. In order to recreate the same situation, you have to be the same person experiencing the situation.

Freud certainly made the basic discoveries here – that people get hung up by childhood traumatic experiences and are compelled to seek out those same experiences all their lives, and that keeping those experiences the same requires keeping the self the same, and so psychological growth is arrested. I don't want to get into an argument with scholars here as to who discovered what. This is all my personal knowledge, from my own personal experience, and I am just trying to give Freud proper credit for his discoveries.

And Freud discovered that the way to resolve these traumatic experiences was to put his patients in a nonjudgmental situation and try to find clues to their subconscious contents through free association and dream analysis. Once the problem was revealed, the adult with the adult's mind was then better able to resolve it than the child was. My psychiatrist also keyed on my psychological defenses, especially rationalization. If I was arguing too much or too strenuously, he would point that out to me and lead me to wonder what I was defending.

Rationalization is only one of the psychological defenses, also known as "ego defenses," discovered by Freud and his daughter Anna. Actually the list of possible psychological defenses is infinite. They are anything that a clever mind can come up with. My definition of "rationalization" applies to all psychological defenses: "Psychological defenses" are arguments which are not quite accurate, but are accurate enough to be believed by somebody that really wants to believe them.

People thought that "psychological defenses" were a device used by Freud to win arguments. Psychological defenses are obviously false arguments to anybody but the person who has them. People need to discover their own psychological defenses in order to know that they are real.

The Hippies made the big splash rejecting psychotherapy, but they borrowed their slogan from the academic people, who had had it for years. Not only the Hippies, and not only the intellectuals, and not only in America, but clever people all over the world rejected Freud. The collective psychological defenses of the entire world rejected Freud.

People who have successfully been through psychotherapy and have recognized the subtlety and power of their own psychological defenses will understand instantly how psychological defenses rejected Freud. People who have not been through psychotherapy will not understand.

The subtlety of psychological defenses is such that people don't even know that they have them. Their power is such that people would rather blow up the world than relax their psychological defenses.

To understand the power and subtlety of psychological defenses, it is not enough to have read about these things in a book. You need to have uncovered some of your own defenses. You need to have been through psychotherapy yourself, with some degree of success.

For this and many other reasons, you will understand better what I am saying in this book if you have been through psychotherapy yourself. Much of what I am saying in this book is a result of having been through psychotherapy, as I experienced it. You will relate to it better if you have been through psychotherapy yourself.

Also, if you have achieved psychological maturity, either naturally or through psychotherapy, you will be better able to understand the differentiations I make in this book. Through psychotherapy, as I became psychologically more mature, I became better able to differentiate, or see the difference. In its higher state this becomes discernment, or the ability to see fine distinctions.

And you will need some psychological maturity to be able to deal with the scary stuff that is really out there, and not instantly ridicule it away, as our culture has done.

These are only a few of the reasons why you will understand this book better if you have had some successful psychotherapy. There are many more.

If I were giving a course in differential equations, I would expect my readers to have knowledge of differential and integral calculus. In the same way, it would help if readers of this book have been through psychotherapy with positive results.

There is another important reason why you need some success at psychotherapy. I didn't find personal happiness or my formula for survival of the species just by going to a psychiatrist. I found these things by analyzing my own dreams. But I learned the disciplines that enabled me to analyze my own dreams in psychotherapy.

Just the idea that the client has to learn disciplines to succeed at psychotherapy is foreign to our culture. The therapist is seen as an authority figure who is going to solve your problem. But no, you have all the information in your own head, although much of it is subconscious. The therapist is only a guide, who can help you get to it, similar to the sherpa who can help you climb Mt. Everest, but you have to climb the mountain.

One thing bothered me, when I read all those books telling me how the brilliant doctor had made a brilliant diagnosis: If that was the diagnosis, then what was the cure?

I didn't learn until I was in therapy myself that this "medical model" was incorrect. It wasn't the case of a diagnosis and a cure at all. It was a case of a problem (or problems) to be solved. When the problem was solved, it went away.

The client has to do the analysis, and the client has to solve the problem. If the brilliant doctor gives the client the solution before the client is ready to accept it, the client's defenses will reject it.

So there are disciplines the client must learn in order to solve his or her own problems, just as there are disciplines one must learn in order to be able to climb Mt. Everest or solve differential equations.

And once these disciplines are learned, one can use them to get an education from one's dreams, as I did. I have the idea, just as a hypothesis, that one cannot develop in therapy beyond the personal philosophy of the therapist. For example, my psychiatrist didn't believe in the spiritual, so I didn't develop the spiritual side of myself while I was with him. But one's dreams are not limited by anybody's personal philosophy, and immediately my dreams began introducing me to the spiritual.

So I am proposing dream analysis as the ultimate education, but only after one has learned the necessary disciplines to succeed at psychotherapy.

Unfortunately, Freud went out of fashion in 1973. It is unlikely that any psychotherapist practicing today would have learned very much about Freud. Fortunately, if you search the Internet for "psychodynamic therapists in my area" or in your state, you will find quite a few. Psychodynamic psychotherapy is the kind of therapy that was pioneered by Freud, focusing on childhood traumatic experiences as the root cause of adult psychological problems.

The primary qualification for the therapist is that he or she has successfully been through therapy himself or herself, although I was never brazen enough to ask the question. You want a sherpa who has personally climbed this mountain before. This used to be a necessary qualification for a psychotherapist, but now it seems that the intellectuals have won out and downplayed its importance. But the whole idea of the brilliant doctor making the brilliant diagnosis and taking credit for the cure, or the therapist thinking that he or she is "better" than the client because he or she has credentials, is ego-compensation on the part of the therapist. The therapist needs to see himself or herself in the role of servant, like the sherpa. These ego-compensations build up resentments in the mind of the client, who is being used by the therapist, and contribute to the failure of psychotherapy.

You need a licensed psychotherapist. You do not want any "alternative" therapy. Doing any unlicensed "alternative" therapy is a psychological defense to avoid the real thing. All the psychodynamic therapists I found on the Internet seemed to be licensed, but check it out and make sure.

And of course get references from people you know, if you can. Say "A friend of mine needs psychotherapy" if you don't want to let on that it is for yourself.

Psychotherapy is expensive. Don't be fooled by the economy of group therapy. It will subject you to the same kind of social pressures that created the problems in the first place.

A single person with a good job should be able to afford psychotherapy, as I did. Married couples with good jobs and no children should also be able to afford it. If you are raising children, try to explore your own inner child first.

It takes humility just to seek the help of a psychotherapist, and even more humility to recognize the unpleasant aspects of yourself that you would rather avoid.

It takes courage to face down the monsters of the deep that are jealously guarding those aspects of your real self that do not want to be discovered.

I have a talent for solving problems. I have actually earned money by solving so-called "impossible" problems. But psychotherapy, at the time, was the most difficult thing I had ever done in my life. And likewise, analyzing my own dreams, in its time, was the most difficult thing I had ever done in my life. I think the main reason for this difficulty is that the same mind that has the problems has to solve the problems. For this reason, it is important to have the other person, the therapist, or the dreams, to keep you focused on the reality. Another important reason for the difficulty of psychotherapy was that I (and others who succeeded at psychotherapy) had to discover things that the professionals did not yet know, such as the fact that the client has to solve the problem. Hopefully, psychotherapy today is more advanced than it was in the 1960s, especially in the art of getting around the client's psychological defenses.

MY ULTIMATE PHILOSOPHY

This book is my ultimate philosophy – not THE ultimate philosophy, but only MY ultimate philosophy, the best that I am able to do in this lifetime, while my mind is still working well. To my surprise, in my old age, I am having a great many new ideas. I have a pretty good idea of what I want to say in this book, but no idea of the new ideas that are going to enhance it as I go along.

In 1955, when I was 21 years old, I saw the threat of nuclear annihilation as proof of total systems failure, not of the technology, but of a culture that could be so stupid as to create the means for its own destruction and possibly the extinction of the whole human species. For the sake of the survival of the species and for my own personal happiness, I turned my back on the culture and set out to design a new civilization, to figure it all out again from scratch, to see if I could get it right.

As it turned out, the methods that enabled me to find personal happiness and a way for the species to survive were psychotherapy as I experienced it, withdrawal from the culture, and analysis of my own dreams. I had my answers by 1967, and was able to produce a manuscript, "The Mental Scene," in 1970. But because the Hippies were the only defined market for such a book, I was rejected by all publishers. I spent years rewriting the book and finally published it myself in 1985 with the title *Re-Educating Myself: An Introduction to a New Civilization.*

I have also written and self-published *The Mental Environment: (Mostly about Mind Pollution)* (2007), describing the network of lies from which I had to extricate myself in my quest for a new civilization, and *Dirty Science: How Unscientific Methods Are Blocking Our Cultural Advancement* (2018), describing how prejudices within the academic community are blocking our culture from knowledge of the psychic and the spiritual. This present book does not replace what I have said in any of my previous books. They stand on their own. I am only building on the structure that I have already created with them.

Re-Educating Myself was my magnum opus, documenting my journey of exploration beyond the mental confines of the culture, in my quest for a new civilization. But as I have read it over and over again in recent years, to produce the Second Edition and the audiobook, I saw how innocent I had been when I wrote it. I had been led to believe, when I was at Harvard, that academic people were open-minded, unbiased, and impartial, unlike religious people, who had prejudices. I thought that academic people would judge the book impartially on its merits, even the merits of turning one's back on the culture, to see where the culture had gone wrong. I thought that these academic people, again impartially, would evaluate the contribution I had made to the culture.

I had no idea that I was exploring in areas that were taboo in the academic subculture – Sigmund Freud, Carl Jung, psychotherapy as education, dream analysis, psychic abilities, the spiritual and spiritual entities, Edgar Cayce, reincarnation, karma, levitation, Richard Kieninger, the Brotherhoods, and Black Mentalists. Even the study of the mind had been abandoned by psychologists. I had the find out about these taboos in what I call "My Second Voyage of Exploration."

Caroline McCullagh, in her review of the Second Edition of *Re-Educating Myself* for the *Mensa Bulletin* (June 2022), said: "I think it's not possible to turn your back on your own culture…" The problem with that is that I never defined what I meant by "turning my back on the culture." It was a symbolic statement. One would have to read the book, and see what I actually did, to know what I meant by it. There is no evidence that she read any of the book.

Intellectuals have argued that I didn't turn my back on the culture, because I went through psychotherapy and read books that were part of the culture. Again, they need to read what I actually did. Obviously, I did not reject everything the culture had taught me.

But now that I have been challenged and forced to think about it, yes, I did turn my back on the culture right away by making my own mind the highest authority to decide for myself what to believe, instead of believing on the basis of some external "authority." This was clearly a violation of cultural norms. People called me "arrogant." This really goes deeper than books or methods. Then, on the basis of my own supreme authority, I decided which books to read and which methods to follow.

When I turned my back on the culture, I envisioned "the culture" as the 7 million books in Widener Library at Harvard at the time. But actually it went deeper than that. What I really turned my back on, unknowingly, was the academic subculture that studied those books and represented or pretended to represent "the culture."

Widener Library has the Bollingen Series by Carl Jung, and the Dartmouth Library has *There Is a River*, the biography of Edgar Cayce, by Thomas Sugrue, *The Ultimate Frontier*, by Richard Kieninger and the Brotherhoods, writing under the pen name of Eklal

Kueshana, and every issue of the *Journal of Parapsychology*, but academic people are given the social signals that they aren't supposed to read these things, if they want to remain socially accepted as members of the academic community.

Those academic people we trust to preserve our cultural knowledge and teach it to others aren't reading or teaching all of it. I had already learned from my grandmother about reincarnation and occult sources of knowledge. I had to learn about Carl Jung from a Provincetown artist. Another artist friend taught me about the Brotherhoods. I learned about Edgar Cayce from a girlfriend of mine. I learned about Richard Kieninger from a student in my Dream Analysis class. None of these people or things were learned about from the academic community.

There is also the view that "the culture" is what the academic subculture says it is, and that all real knowledge has to come through them. This view is implanted in the minds of two million college graduates each year and thus becomes part of the larger culture. It is supported by the "straw-man" argument that the so-called "self-made man" did not write all the books or invent the language, and is therefore not entirely self-made. But the self-made man has studied the reality, independently of the academic view of it. There is a reality independent of how the academic establishment views it. By studying this reality directly, and not just as it was taught by the academic establishment, I turned my back on the view that has been disseminated through our culture, that all knowledge comes from or through the academic establishment. The academic establishment does have a monopoly, but not on the truth.

I also turned my back on the idea that knowledge came from books. Yes, I read some books, as information, as I have explained. But mainly I studied the reality. That was the real authority (no quotes). What I read in books had to agree with the reality, as I experienced it, and not the other way around.

I have also heard that Freud said that it was impossible to break free of one's culture. Again, what exactly he meant by that was not defined. Certainly, I have no desire to break free of owning a car, or living in a comfortable house, or taking advantage of any of the material comforts my culture offers me. But I think just the fact that I have had to create expressions such as "psychological age," "the psychological age of puberty," "the moose principle," "the self-steering process," and "the mental senses" to describe things that were not known to the culture is sufficient evidence to show that I broke free of my culture.

Psychotherapy helped me to break free of the Establishment and assert my real self in the face of cultural pressures to be something I wasn't. Withdrawal made me "strange," even more independent of cultural pressures. But the thing that really enabled me to break free of my culture was the education I received from interpreting my own dreams. This was the greatest wisdom I have ever experienced in my life, and it came from a source that was independent of the culture, a more universal view of things.

What Freud said was impossible was possible for me. Actually, Freud broke free of his culture with his many discoveries, so I have been fed misinformation.

Further proof that I broke free of my culture is that people with academic credentials couldn't seem to read the same words that I wrote in *Re-Educating Myself.* It was beyond their ken. They tried to make it into something they could understand and fit into their belief structure, with the attitude, "We know everything; therefore this has to be something we know already." It just didn't seem to register with them that this was a whole other belief system and a whole other culture.

I am reminded of the time I was playing a little "Arab" tune I had composed, with 7 beats to a measure, and my friend, an excellent musician, was trying to drum along with me. He didn't believe that it was 7 beats to a measure, because it swung right along – sounded very normal. He was sure it was 8 beats to a measure. So he would start drumming and then stop when he got out of sync, thinking he had made a mistake somewhere, and still believing it had to be 8 beats to a measure.

And so it is with *Re-Educating Myself.* It swings right along. It all looks very familiar. But it isn't. I will always appreciate the young guy who commented, "You make it look easy." Well, no, I don't, not really. It is only that the intellectuals have made it look difficult.

I think that part of what makes it look easy is the simple language. This is part of what makes psychotherapy a new way of thinking. In psychotherapy, one deals with specifics, not abstract language. Actually, the use of abstract language is seen in psychotherapy as a defense mechanism, because abstract language is ambiguous, unless defined precisely, as in mathematics.

I will get into this more when I discuss academic philosophy. Right now, all I am trying to say is that my use of simple language may have fooled the intellectuals into thinking that the things I am saying aren't very intelligent.

Whatever the explanation is, most people did not understand *Re-Educating Myself.* So I feel that I must present a summary of it here, to give you an idea of where I went and where I am coming from. And just be warned that it is another culture and isn't as familiar as it might look.

CHAPTER 2

Re-Educating Myself

THE BOMB

In the summer of 1953, when I was 19 years old, the Soviet Union exploded their first hydrogen bomb. Up until then, only the United States had had the ultimate weapon. Now two countries in bitter rivalry had the ultimate weapon. ("We will bury you." – Khrushchev) In a few years the word "overkill" was coined, meaning that each country had the capacity to kill all of the enemy many times over. The novel *On the Beach* showed how the radioactive fallout would kill everybody else in the world. *Homo sapiens* had both the means and the motive to exterminate our own species, or at least "Bomb us back to the Stone Age," as the expression was in those days.

The manly virtues of fighting and warfare, which had been instilled into every boy child since before history had begun, and had been instilled into every girl child insofar as she had learned to respect and admire the men who protected her, was now no longer a good thing. It had led us, via the arms race, to a point where we were in danger of exterminating our own species. I realized, as Einstein had already recognized in 1945, "We need a whole new way of thinking."

THE AMERICAN DREAM COMES TRUE

In 1954, when I was 20, I was thinking about what I wanted to do with my adult life. My father and grandfather before me had

worked to make money. I had the advantages of this money –
boats, cars, summer places, and social position. But I wasn't happy
where I was. This was unheard of in America. I was the end prod-
uct of "the American dream." People had come to this country
mostly in poverty, and had worked and suffered so that they could
have money, or at least their children or grandchildren could enjoy
the comforts of having money. And now that I had those comforts,
it was unthinkable that I should not be happy. I had to be some
kind of a punk kid.

This may seem like a personal problem, but it isn't. As our tech-
nology provides more and more people with material comfort,
more and more people are faced with the question, "What else is
there to life?"

Happiness was what I wanted in life. I asked myself who was
the happiest person I knew, and I found my great-aunt Margaret
Seaver, "Tada" to me. It seemed that she didn't have the natural
abilities my parents had, but where my parents had achieved suc-
cess by the cultural standard by using only a part of their natural
abilities, Tada was using a greater part of her human potential and
enjoying a greater happiness as a result.

So I decided that the way to happiness was to develop my po-
tential as a human being. And assuming that I had the same natural
ability as my parents, I realized that in developing my potential I
would go beyond the cultural standard and probably beyond the
ability of the culture even to judge. I envisioned myself as becom-
ing some kind of fabulous weirdo.

"THE WASTE LAND"

In 1955, I studied "The Waste Land," by T.S. Eliot, ostensibly to
write a paper on some academic question, but actually to answer a
question of my own. "The Waste Land" had been presented to me
in at least two different English courses as the most important ex-
ample of twentieth-century writing, but also it had been presented
as some kind of madness, and we were promised, "This won't be
on the exam." So, then, my question was, "If this is madness, then
why is it important?"

As I studied "The Waste Land," it became more and more de-
pressing:

I think we are in the rats' alley
Where dead men lost their bones.

As I became more familiar with it, I could see that "The Waste Land" was my world. I was living it – boring relationships and the prospect of a meaningless life with endless commutes to meaningless jobs. The old religious beliefs, which had given us our values, had collapsed, leaving twentieth-century humanity stumbling amidst the rubble of broken images.

This was my first experience of self-knowledge. It was the hardest thing I had ever done in my life, at the time. I had been trained to look outward at an external world – physics, chemistry, history, geography – but never to look inward at myself. In ninth-grade ancient history we had learned that Socrates was a Greek philosopher who said, "Know thyself." These were only words we had to memorize, with no explanation of what they meant.

"The Waste Land" was an instant smash hit when it was first published in 1922. But in 1955, I was seeing the same world that it portrayed. Nobody had done anything about the situation. I was determined that I would do something about the problem. I looked to the poem to see if T.S. Eliot offered a solution. But all he said was:

Shall I at least set my lands in order?

That was no solution. I was the model boy. People respected me and envied me. My lands were in order. It was the world that was a mess.

But the more I thought about it, the more I recognized that it was the most efficient way to change the world. If I try to change another person, our wills clash, and we fight. At least changing myself I had only one will to deal with. And at least I could change one small fraction of the world.

TURNING MY BACK ON THE CULTURE

In 1955, at age 21, for these three reasons – the threat of nuclear annihilation, the need for goals beyond "the American dream," and the need for new values to take us beyond "The Waste Land" – I turned my back on the culture and set out to design a new civilization.

I saw "the culture" as the seven million books at the time in Widener Library at Harvard. I wanted to start all over again at the beginning and figure it all out for myself.

"New civilization" was the best expression I could think of to mean new values, new beliefs, new ideals, new goals, a new "standard of living," a new way of thinking, and a new way of life.

[No, I have never used the word "paradigm." That is somebody else's word in somebody else's book, and just because that book is more famous doesn't mean that my thinking has to fit into the structure it defines.]

The "civilization," to me, was what had been programmed into my head as a product of the American upper middle class. All I had to do to create a new civilization was to change that programming. Of course this is more easily said than done.

I asked myself, "Who am I to be creating a new civilization?" There was nobody expert in this field, so it seemed that it came down to raw intelligence. Maybe I had the highest IQ on record in the Taunton public schools, but at Harvard it seemed I was only about average.

I was pondering this question in 1956, when I applied for Navy Officer Candidate School (OCS). I took their physical and mental exams, and about a week later I got a call from Naval Headquarters in Boston, telling me they wanted to see me.

When I arrived, there were three Naval officers just sitting around. The man at the desk said, "We just wanted to see what you looked like. You got the highest score we have ever seen on the Mental Exam."

This was in competition with students from Harvard and M.I.T. and all the colleges in the Boston area. It seemed I was as well qualified as anybody to be designing a new civilization.

[I now realize that the Navy test was rigged in my favor. In addition to the normal Mathematical and Verbal sections, there was a Mechanical section which tested one's knowledge of boats and the maintenance of boats. I know I got a perfect score on that section, because I had spent all my summers in and around boats and had worked two months in a boatyard. But the Navy was telling me what I wanted to hear at the time, and I went with it.]

On their Medical History Questionnaire, I answered "Yes" to the question, "Are you often depressed?" That led to further examination by a psychiatrist, whose report was favorable. But because the class was oversubscribed, I was rejected because of this "abnormality."

Wiser heads advised me that I should not have answered "Yes" to that question. But I was using the Navy's stringent testing to evaluate myself.

I had been turned down from a job because of my psychological condition. I had had 19 years of intellectual education. Now it seemed that I needed a psychological education. I saw psychotherapy as a necessary part of my education. I was depressed, and also I couldn't rely on my own mind. I saw my mind as like a wild horse with a will of its own, causing me to fail when consciously I wanted to succeed.

But before I could do psychotherapy, I had to spend two years in the Army, under President Eisenhower's Universal Military Training.

I made my own mind the highest authority to decide what to believe. I didn't know, at the time, that I had always had this authority, and that everybody has this authority.

I questioned everything I had ever been taught, starting with "Can I use logic?" By "logic," I mean the human ability to reason and all the formal logic and mathematics built on top of that. And I realized that without logic I could not put on my clothes in the morning, or find food, or find my way home at night. Without logic, I would not know "true" from "false."

I know that there are mystics who try not to use logic, but as long as I am on this earth and dealing with the problems of this earth, I am going to use logic, until it is proved to me logically that logic doesn't work.

Along with logic, I decided to accept what had been scientifically proved – not just the opinions of scientists, but only what had been demonstrated by scientific methods to be true.

I wanted my new civilization to be based upon beliefs that were true. The wisdom of twentieth-century psychology told me, "We believe what we want to believe." People trying to avoid that bias tried to believe in just the opposite – things that were unpleasant to believe, such as unrewarding lives and unsuccessful outcomes. I just wanted to believe in the truth: "I don't care what I believe, as long as it is true." My bias was towards the truth. I was as ruthless in my pursuit of truth as anybody ever was in their pursuit of power or money.

Along with my dedication to the truth, I decided that since warfare was a problem, I would try to live my life without ever doing warfare. I define "warfare" as any destructive act, physical or mental, against another person or persons.

Also I decided to live for the greatest good of humanity and not for the maximum profit for myself. With my intelligence, I could always make enough money to support myself. I saw my intelligence as a gift of God, and not as something I could take credit for myself. Therefore I wanted to use that intelligence to serve what I saw as the best interests of God. Actually, I PRAY that I may live for the good of humanity, because I know that not everybody who thinks they are doing good is really doing good.

So these have been my three operating principles:

dedication to the truth
to never do warfare
to live for the greatest good of humanity

It has always seemed to me that the words of Jesus, "Blessed are the meek; for they shall inherit the earth" (Matthew 5:5), represent a greater truth than warfare. We just haven't figured out yet how that works. The meek are not weak. They are simply people who don't do warfare.

I realized that if I tried to build my system on all the "right" things, I would end up with the same civilization all over again. I had to find my new beliefs from among the things the existing culture considered "wrong." That doesn't mean that I had to reject everything the culture considered "right," or believe things just because they were "wrong." But I had to discover where the culture was wrong in considering things "wrong."

The wrongest thing I could think of was to deny the existence of God. I imagined that whatever my father would do to me if I denied God's existence, God would do worse. But I allowed myself the fullness of the thought, "There is no God," and no thunderbolt came. That didn't mean that there was no God. It could also mean that God allowed me to think that thought. This gave me a great sense of freedom from the dictates of organized religion.

Actually, I was never a serious believer. I learned on the first day of Sunday school that the Christian religion didn't have all the answers.

When I was four years old, I had the conviction that I had always existed. I knew I was just a little boy, four years old, but my conviction was that I had existed much longer than that.

When I was six, my sister June was born. I got the news when I was in play school. And as I was walking home, I was pondering the philosophical question, "A person now exists who didn't exist before. How can that be?"

So I was ready with my question on the first day of Sunday school. The teacher was talking about the life hereafter, and I raised my hand and asked, "Where was I before?"

The teacher's answer was unconvincing, so when I got home, I asked my grandmother the same question.

My grandmother Harriet Seaver was no ordinary grandmother. She was a philosopher, an artist, and a member of the Theosophical Society. Her bookcase was stuffed with ancient and occult wisdom. A couple of her books that I remember reading were *The* [Egyptian] *Book of the Dead* and *The Rosicrucian Cosmo-Conception*. She even had a law degree.

She explained to me that the Hindus believed that we had many lives. That made much more sense to me than the Christian view. But she was also careful to explain to me that this was a Hindu belief, and I was living in a Christian country, and if I wanted to believe it, I should keep it to myself.

So I had gone through my younger years as a sort of halfway Christian, with a belief in God and reincarnation. But as I gave it some thought, I realized that I had been told I had to believe in a God I had never seen and nobody had seen for thousands of years. Consistent with my scientific background, I adopted the working hypothesis, "I will believe in God when I see God."

At one point I was so depressed that I was contemplating suicide. But I quickly realized that that would just be a waste. If I was willing to die, I could turn that into a source of power. If I was willing to die, I could endure any lesser pain, fear, or humiliation in pursuit of my goals. With my dedication to the truth, I became a fanatic on a suicide mission.

To most people these days this means "terrorist," because that's the kind of suicide mission that we hear about on the news. But there is an important difference. Here you have to be able to differentiate. I didn't want to kill people or do them any harm. I was only willing to risk harm or death to myself to achieve my goals.

By 1957, people were running around screaming, "Save the world !!!" Many of us set out to save the world. I saw it as an activity "worth my sweat." We were labeled "The Silent Generation." I hated that. The threat of nuclear annihilation was enough of a problem to silence anybody. It was not a problem that could be solved right away. Maybe in 10 years I could find a solution.

WHILE I WAS IN THE ARMY

During my two years in a peacetime Army, I did an enormous amount of reading, mostly psychology, but also philosophy, good fiction, and factual material – anything I wanted to read, and anything I didn't want to read.

I even tried to psychoanalyze myself, but that didn't work. I just found myself going around in bigger and bigger circles. I needed that other person to keep me focused.

When I was in Basic Training, most of my buddies had not been to college, but I found that I could have meaningful conversations with them, even on the deepest philosophical subjects, if I just didn't use the big words I had learned in college.

And what good are the big words, anyway? A big word that many people were using in those days was "existentialism." But no two people that I talked to ever had the same definition of it. So what good is this word?

I decided that it meant that twentieth-century thinkers were able to assert "I exist," after people had been forced into artificial roles by society for centuries. I will spare you the convoluted definition in my dictionary. But unless we all have the same definition, what use is the word?

In the Army, I learned a brainstorming technique that was valuable to me in my psychological development. I call it "scribbling." I think it is similar to what James Pennebaker has called "traumatic journaling." You just write down whatever is on your mind. Nobody else is ever going to read this. Let it all out. No need for correct spelling or grammar.

This was helpful to me in the Army, because the Army was a horrible place for me and the other college graduates I was stationed with, in involuntary servitude. We had a saying in our barracks, "In 20 years you'll look back on this and you'll still be mad." So I didn't want to dump my bad feelings on my buddies and increase their bad feelings. And I didn't want to dump these bad feelings on anybody outside, like a girlfriend. So the perfect solution was to dump them on a piece of paper, which I could then just dump into the waste basket.

One day I started off just writing "Shit, shit, shit, shit, shit, …" until I got tired of it. And then I was surprised that my mind then turned to clear philosophical thoughts. It was like mentally having a bowel movement. The act of writing the thoughts on paper cleaned them out of my system, whereas if I had just let them stay there, they would have poisoned me forever.

When I was in the Army, my grandmother broke her hip and was confined to bed. I saw this as similar to my confinement in the Army, and I felt an empathy with her. I tried to write her encouraging letters, but at age 23, I had a whole life ahead of me, whereas at 83, what did she have to look forward to? Her hip was replaced and she could have gotten out of bed, but she didn't want to. After several months of being bedridden, she hardly spoke a coherent sentence to anybody.

But one weekend when I came home, she sat upright in a chair and had an articulate discussion of philosophy with me for an hour and a half. At the end, she said to me, "I am surprised that you know these things already." I was surprised, too. I hypothesized that in that conversation she had given me her most valuable possession, her knowledge of philosophy, or at least some part of it, by direct mental communication.

As her condition deteriorated, I was in empathy with her. On Easter Sunday of 1958, I was totally depressed. By Tuesday, I was so depressed that I couldn't get up out of bed, and I had to ask a buddy to pick up my legs and put them on the floor. At noon, I had a quick lunch and took a quick nap and had the following dream:

Sort of family gathering, dark hall, waiting for dinner – like Thanksgiving, except Friday <u>after</u> Easter. My mother waiting to say grace. Buffet dinner on *high table, children's table off to left. I remembered the same table from some-where before. Many unidentified relatives, uncles, men, waiting to enter door.*

My grandmother and Tada sitting at table next to each other. My grand-mother mentioning old relatives. Says she wants to go to Louisiana or visit Aunt Louisa. She looks very cheery and young – Tada more or less ignoring her chatter because it is meaningless, saying "You know Aunt Louisa is ----," omitting mention of death.

My grandmother gets up from the table, stares out the dining-room window, and then goes out the door to the living room, which is now the back gate, leading out into a yard. It looks like Uncle Ed's house, but with long court-yards in back. Some of the guests hadn't arrived – I think she was going to get them. I knew that she would not come back – her health was too poor – and started running after her. I run through first courtyard gate. She disappears. She is now a skinny little 12-year-old, running very fast through gate at other end (100 feet or so away).

My father yells from behind me, "Don't go on a marathon, Bob," (or something like that) at which point I stop to turn back and notice people of all ages and sizes, coming the other way from the opposite gate. Most of them are under 30. I start running, nearly colliding with thirtyish young man in brown suit, then notice my grandmother coming out cellar door which was the maids' quarters, saying, "The dinner is ready. Everything will be all right," (or some-thing like that) at which point she returns to the table, looking thirtyish and dressed in Victorian costume of the early century – hair reddish brown, eyes blue, and slightly plumper.

Quick scene shift from dining room to front of house (again similar to Uncle Ed's – stucco house, surrounded by stucco walls) and saw young kid with man's face, dressed in black cowboy hat, red shirt, blue jeans, with six-guns. Somebody remarked that he was quite an up-and-coming young man. He had a Russian name (Alexy Karamazov? Alfred? Alexandroff?), came from Wellfleet. I sensed him as a competitor.

This was obviously about my grandmother's death. But all I knew about dreams at the time was Freudian wish-fulfillment. I wished she would die? The whole family wished she would die? Actually, she herself, it seemed, wanted to die. But that didn't seem to explain the dream, and it was time to get back to work.

When I arrived in the office, my boss said, "There's a telegram for you at the Message Center."

The hair stood up on the back of my neck. She had died, at 9:15 that morning. The funeral would be on Friday, the Friday after

Easter. The dream had reached me with the message before the telegram.

It also happened that the funeral service was in the dining room, because it was the most convenient place for the funeral director to set up the chairs, just by removing the table.

This one dream was all the evidence I ever needed, to prove the physicalists wrong. There was more to reality than I had learned in all my physics courses at Harvard.

The physicalists would argue that I just happened to have this dream, at this time, by coincidence. I wasted a lot of time in *Re-Educating Myself* arguing that there were huge odds against having this particular dream at this particular time by chance. It was the only dream I had ever had about my grandmother's death, it was the most powerful dream that I had had in a long time, and I only had time for one dream between the time of my grandmother's death and the time I was aware of the telegram. But it didn't matter to the physicalists if there was only one chance in 100,000 of having this particular dream at this particular time. To them, the chances of having this communication by telepathy were zero.

But they have a bias, enforced by the threat of losing their professional careers if they deviate from it. And I have no such bias. Yes, they can ridicule me, but they know that that is not a legitimate argument. I am free to take the explanation that is the most reasonable: My grandmother (or the whole family) communicated with me by telepathy at the time of her death, and I became conscious of it later in my dream.

MY PSYCHOTHERAPY

Soon after getting out of the Army, I moved to New York, and with the help of friends found a good psychiatrist.

My experience with psychotherapy refutes the charge that nobody ever got well with Freudian methods. The fact that I went through the basic process designed by Freud and achieved the desired results is hard evidence that the system works. I resent the fact that I have to display my own private experience with psychotherapy to refute these people. I'm sure there are thousands or millions of people whose lives have been changed by Freud's methods. I am going to summarize here those aspects of Freud's methods, as updated to 1959, that I have tested in my life's experience and found accurate.

I lay on a couch and talked to the ceiling. My psychiatrist sat behind me, out of sight. This helped me to say accurately what was on my mind. I am distracted when I have to face people and look them in the eye.

My psychiatrist took an active part in the discussion. This is in contrast to another form of therapy where the therapist hardly ever says anything.

My psychiatrist maintained absolute confidentiality. He had double doors so that I could never hear what another patient was saying.

He maintained a nonjudgmental environment, so that I knew I could tell him anything without him giving me a moral lecture. One time I had an unfavorable insight into myself, and I asked myself, "Do I want him to hear this?" And I realized that I didn't mind if he heard it, but I didn't want to admit it to MYSELF.

He had me write down my dreams and bring them in. Dreams were important. He taught me to look for the headline in a dream, as a newspaper would give it. One dream I had, where I brushed my father's leg with my foot under the table, he gave the headline, "SON KICKS FATHER." That's the way dreams are. They are mildly suggestive of something, so that the audience won't walk out in indignation and close down the theater.

He trained me to be an observer of myself and my own mental processes. For a great many sessions he had me tell him everything in detail I had done and thought, from the time I got up in the morning.

He had me speak in specific terms. This is an aspect of psychotherapy that makes it a new way of thinking, in sharp contrast to the abstractions used in Western academic philosophy and most of the academic world. For example, Freud's theory has been called "deterministic," but does that mean that childhood experiences CAN determine adult behavior, or that childhood experiences ALWAYS DO determine adult behavior, or that childhood experiences ARE THE SOLE DETERMINANT of adult behavior? There is an ambiguity in the abstraction, and people can slide from one definition to another. Using specific language is more accurate than using abstractions.

My psychiatrist kept me focused on "the reality." The reality that he believed in didn't include the spiritual, so I just avoided that subject. But the idea that there is a reality independent of my belief is essential to psychotherapy. If the reality can be anything I believe in, then it is OK to be crazy, and psychotherapy isn't going to work.

What did I gain from psychotherapy?

As I shed myself of my childhood self, I became less vulnerable to the "authority hooks," which had made me obey every time a person gave me a command. I also became less suggestible, or less vulnerable to hypnotic command.

I hadn't thought of myself as a manipulator, but psychotherapy made me aware of my manipulations.

The subconscious is not a fixed place in the mind. As I brought subconscious things into consciousness, I was actually converting the subconscious into consciousness – rolling back the shade of the subconscious, as I saw it. I became aware that before psychotherapy I had lived in a semi-conscious state, not really being aware of things.

From out of the subconscious, I discovered mental abilities I didn't know I had. The first was creativity. Before psychotherapy, I couldn't imagine writing an original song. All the combinations of 7 notes surely had been written. But after psychotherapy, I wrote several songs, the best of which were published as *Uncle Bobby's Record* (1974) and later republished by Old Bear Records.

I discovered intuition, that analog function of the mind, as contrasted to the digital function, which is the intellect. I was arguing something one day with my psychiatrist, when suddenly I "saw," in a flash, the truth of everything he was saying.

Psychologists claim that intuition is false in children. That may be so, but in adult life I have found intuition to be very accurate. I always check it with my intellect. Intuition was a great asset in interpreting my dreams – "playing my hunches."

The third mental aspect I uncovered was my will. The will is doing what I want, as opposed to "willpower," which is doing what I really don't want to do. Of course the will, the "I want," is totally suppressed in the child, because what society wants us to do is totally superior to what we want to do. But I see it as a defining aspect of the great creative people, who take the attitude, "I don't care what you want or think you want. This is what I am going to give you."

We all grow up as kids, and as kids we are inferior. Grownups are bigger, stronger, and more knowledgeable. They have the authority, they have the money, and they own the house. We get the idea at a very early age that we are inferior, and psychotherapy helps us grow out of that.

As I matured psychologically, I was better able to differentiate, or know the difference. Another word for this is "discriminate," but "discriminate" is more often used to mean not being able to differentiate, as in prejudices against the out-group – (all X are Y). The ability to differentiate is really the key to psychological development.

And my sex life improved.

All of these things contributed to my happiness. I came out of my depression about 10 months after I started therapy and never went back. Every month when I paid my psychiatrist's bill, I asked myself, "What have I gained THIS MONTH (not THIS YEAR or FROM THE BEGINNING) to justify paying this much money?" And every month I saw significant gains that were well worth it.

I have put Freud to the test in my real-life experience and found that his core system was accurate. Children have traumatic experiences, situations they are unable to deal with emotionally because they don't have the brain power, the experience, or the knowledge. These experiences, because of the way the mind works, cause them to become "arrested." They preserve the self at the same level of development in order to experience the same situation again, and they seek out the same situation until they resolve it.

These traumatic experiences are in fact resolved by putting them in a confidential and non-judgmental setting and engaging them in conversation, keying on their defense mechanisms, free associations, and dreams to give clues to where the problem areas lie. This has worked for me, to free me up from these problems and develop my mind in areas that I did not know existed until I had psychotherapy. I consider psychotherapy to have been about equal in value to my Harvard education, for about the same amount of money. (Now it would cost about the same as one year at Harvard.)

Freud made many mistakes, but those mistakes were not in his core system. And of course the things he got wrong do not invalidate the things he got right.

The greatest of his mistakes was not believing in the spiritual. My psychiatrist did not believe in the spiritual, either. He believed "Religion is a crutch for weak minds." (In those days, religion was all we knew about the spiritual.) So I just avoided any discussion of the spiritual with him. There were plenty of mundane issues to resolve without getting into the spiritual.

Freud's pupil Carl Jung of course got into the spiritual, and what did it get him? He was branded as a "mystic" and rejected. So Freud's denial of the spiritual was actually necessary for him to be accepted by Western civilization in the early twentieth century.

Freud insisted that all psychological problems had to do with sex. Actually, my main traumatic problem had to do with violence and anger. Betrayal also was a major factor in three of my childhood traumas. Jung tried to correct Freud on this.

Freud saw the subconscious as a garbage dump for unwanted memories, thoughts, and feelings. Jung saw this, too, but also saw the subconscious as a source of creative ideas and spiritual inspiration.

Freud saw dreams accurately as "the royal road to the unconscious." But his view of dreams as "wish-fulfillment" was not accurate. Jung's view of dreams as "a compensation for, or correction to, the conscious attitude" is more accurate. I don't think we understand yet what dreams really are.

Freud talked about "infantile sexuality." I didn't experience sexuality until puberty.

The "Oedipus complex," I believe, has nothing to do with sex, but is the child's (male or female) desire to possess the mother.

Freud was the pioneer of psychotherapy, just as Hippocrates was the pioneer of medicine. I see psychotherapy 100 years after Freud as comparable to medicine 100 years after Hippocrates. We can't expect it to be perfect.

Just as Jung made improvements to Freud's thinking, I had to make some discoveries of my own, in order to succeed at psychotherapy. Most of this I have said before, but I think it is worth saying again, because I don't think it is part of the cultural awareness.

First of all, I had to correct "the medical model." The medical model had been fed to us to get away from the stigma that people with psychological problems were possessed by demons and therefore morally to be despised. The medical model taught that having psychological problems was just like being sick. It wasn't people's fault if they were sick. That didn't work. The stigma has stayed with psychological problems, even though it is only thought of as being "sick."

Under the medical model, all the psychology books I had read described how the brilliant doctor had made a brilliant diagnosis. But they never explained what was the cure.

In psychotherapy, I learned that it wasn't a diagnosis and a cure, but a problem to be solved. When the problem was solved, it went away. And it wasn't enough for the brilliant doctor to solve the problem. The client had to solve the problem.

The client has all the information in his or her own head, whether conscious or unconscious. The therapist doesn't know any of this. The therapist is not some "authority" who can tell clients what their problems are. The therapist is only a guide who can read the signs through the clients' defenses, dreams, and free associations, to take them to the areas where their problems lie. The clients have to identify the problems and solve them. The clients have buried these problems because they are accompanied by unpleasant emotions – pain, fear, and/or anger. The clients' psychological defenses protect them from this unpleasantness. If the brilliant doctor tries to give the client the solution before the client is ready to accept it, the client's defenses will reject it. So. basically, the client has to do the analysis, and the client has to solve the problem.

This flies in the face of the medical model and our whole authoritarian orientation. When I am on the operating table, I am just a piece of meat, and the doctor does all the work. So people think that the therapist is going to solve the problem. Whether this attitude is held just by the general public, or whether it is shared by therapists as well, I don't know. But my sarcasm about the "brilliant" doctor reflects an attitude I saw in the literature. The therapists were taking the credit. The therapists were putting themselves in the position of "authorities" because they had the credentials. No, the therapists are in the position of "sherpa," but the client has to climb the mountain.

I succeeded at psychotherapy because I am a good problem-solver. Still, it was the hardest thing I had ever done in my life, at the time. My experience at figuring out "The Waste Land" definitely helped, as an introduction to self-knowledge.

On my part, I helped the process by looking for the fault or the ulterior motive in everything I did. For example, if my boss did something horrendous to me, his fault didn't matter. I was at fault for being angry at him, for expecting him to be perfect, the idealized parental authority figure (IPAF).

When the Hippies came along, they were to label this attitude of mine "negativity" and make it taboo. But for me, this attitude has been the key to my whole psychological growth process. How else can a person learn except by becoming aware of one's faults?

Before I began psychotherapy, I wrote in my scribbling, "Let the dragon kill St. George. Throw away the old Bob Gebelein." With this attitude, I was ready to move in the face of fear, as was necessary in psychotherapy.

In my first therapy session, I told the psychiatrist, "I am very intelligent. I can do this quickly."

It was not a very intelligent thing to say. Psychotherapy is a mental growth process. It is not the same as learning things in school. It is more like learning a skill, such as learning to play a sport or a musical instrument.

My psychiatrist did not believe I was very intelligent, or at least acted as if he didn't believe. He treated it as if it were a fantasy of mine.

After a few weeks, he sent me to a psychologist for psychological testing, which included intelligence testing. I was having so much fun playing with the blocks that I probably didn't do it quickly enough, but when I was able to remember a 9-digit number backwards, the psychologist asked me how I did that.

This, of course, established my intelligence scientifically with my psychiatrist. But then he told me that high intelligence was actually a detriment to psychotherapy, because it enabled a person to create better defenses and rationalizations.

It seemed that he had made this whole production – not believing my intelligence and then sending me to a psychologist to verify it – to make this one important point, and I repeat: High intelligence can be a detriment to psychotherapy.

One of the most intelligent men I have known went to a prominent New York therapist, because his wife was threatening to leave him if he didn't, and at the end of the session decided, "I can be a psychotherapist," and went up to Columbia to sign up for courses. Some psychological defenses are truly brilliant.

Similar to the issue of my intelligence, I had to prove things to my psychiatrist as if I was arguing a case in court. For example, as I was walking down the street one day, I saw an angry man, and that made me angry.

My psychiatrist said, "You didn't know that that man was angry. You only knew that you were angry."

I didn't know at the time that the angry man was the key to my main traumatic experience. I only respected my psychiatrist's good logic.

As a problem-solver, I have a different view of depression than the cultural view. Depression, to me, is the pain of having an unsolved problem. When I solve the problem, the pain goes away. I have experienced this not only with psychological problems but also with difficult problems in my work. The way out of depression for me was to do exactly what I felt like doing – going to sleep. Lots and lots of sleep was what I needed for my mind to function at its best. I am not saying I resolved my childhood traumatic experiences this way, in one supreme effort, but at least it helped, one step at a time.

This is something my psychiatrist taught me: You don't leap the staircase in one bound. You take it one step at a time. I didn't go from a person with a poor self-image and many ego-compensations and fantasies to a person with high self-esteem overnight. It took me years of hard work.

I don't know of any nice neat linear solutions to solve the problems of life. The way I solved my problems was via an iterative solution, getting closer and closer approximations to the truth. When I was in the Army, trying to psychoanalyze myself, I just found myself going around in bigger and bigger circles, and thought that was no good. But as I began to make progress in psychotherapy, I still found myself going around in huge circles, with one important difference: As I came around to each subject again, I found that I understood it a little better than on the previous time around. I was not going around in circles, but in an ascending spiral.

In the spring of 1959, a short time after I began therapy, I was trying to find the real "me." And I discovered that my real self, my favorite self, the self I identified with, was my 4 year old self. Much of what I had been and done after age 4 had been an act, playing the role of whatever I thought a person my age would be doing or saying. So of course I had anxieties, and of course I was depressed, now at age 24, trying to find a job in New York City and trying to have relationships with adult women.

I formulated the concept of "psychological age" and saw myself as "psychological age 4."

"Psychological age" is the level of psychological (emotional, behavioral, philosophical) development that a person is capable of at a given age. It is a measure of a person's mental potential at a given age.

"Psychological development" means creating the circuitry in our minds to channel the raw energy of the drives into appropriate behavior. It begins when we are born, when we are just one bundle of raw, undifferentiated energy. It is the most important human creative activity – not art, architecture, music, literature, or dance, but the creation of a human being.

As we grow, our physical brains develop. Our intelligence increases as a result. That is measured as IQ. But also we are gaining in experience and knowledge, and as our total mental ability grows, we are better able to create the circuitry to channel the raw energy of our drives into appropriate behavior.

"Appropriate behavior" is the goal of psychotherapy – to behave in every situation in such a way that it comes out most favorably for us.

The best example of appropriate behavior was Martin Luther King, Jr. He didn't try to fight back against the people who were oppressing him. And he didn't subordinate himself to their power, either. He did exactly what was necessary to win his civil rights and those of millions of others.

So when I say I was "psychological age 4," it means that my behavior was determined by the mental potential I had at age 4.

I have read books on "EQ" (the emotional equivalent of "IQ") and "emotional intelligence." They aren't talking about the exact same thing as I am talking about, because they include the ability to manipulate people, or "Machiavellianism," in their definition. Psychological development as I experienced it includes ethical considerations of how we treat other people. I didn't like myself as a manipulator, and I liked myself a lot better when I stopped doing that.

[Richard Kieninger also used the concept of "emotional age" or "psychological age," changing from one expression to the other at about the same time as I did. He didn't publish a book until 1963, and I didn't read anything he wrote until 1971, so at least I can say that I formulated the concept of "psychological age" independently.]

Of course I wasn't totally at a 4-year-old level. I was physically a man, six feet tall. I had reached an adult level of performance in mathematics, baseball, sailing, music, and many other things. I had graduated from Harvard, had served honorably in the Army, had been hired out of 75 applicants for my first job in New York, where I discovered on the first day of work that I had a talent for computer programming, and did so well at the job that I became a legend at that company after I left. I could have had a successful career as a computer programmer at psychological age 4. It was only a small aspect of me that was psychological age 4, and that small aspect was not visible to other people except in certain emotional situations.

And so we have the concept of the "inner child," which has been minimized and ridiculed by a culture that wants to believe they are adult. My psychiatrist went along with my concept of psychological age, even though it wasn't part of his culture at the time (only Freud's and Erikson's stages were known), and helped me to bring up the child.

Psychotherapy was the preferred method for personal growth before the Drug Revolution. When I was undergoing psychotherapy in the years 1959 to 1963, most of my friends in New York were also in therapy. We shared the knowledge and language of psychotherapy, being intimately aware, from first-hand experience, of such things as ulterior motives, defense mechanisms, ego compensation, and so forth. The New School for Social Research in New York actually offered psychotherapy for credit in the 1960s.

I know I have said this before, but the culture wants to forget it, so I have to keep reminding you of it.

After three and a half years, my psychiatrist told me I was OK, I was normal, and I could end the treatment. But I still felt dependent on him, so I stayed on for another year, until my company moved me to California.

I certainly felt OK, normal, and comfortable as an adult. But despite my improved psychological condition, I felt there was something missing.

The fact that I successfully completed psychotherapy to the satisfaction of my psychiatrist and made substantial gains in my personal happiness, using the basic principles of Freudian depth psychology, should refute all the Freud-bashers. Yes, Freud made many mistakes. And maybe he was a horrible person. But his basic system was sound, and revolutionized Western thinking. It was, as a boss of mine once described it, "The greatest technological innovation since the cave man."

THE SOCIAL LAWS

In 1964, I bought the book *Human Behavior: An Inventory of Scientific Findings*, by Bernard Berelson and Gary A. Steiner, which outlined scientific findings in psychology and sociology. Among its "1,045 conclusions about human conduct" were some observations about group behavior, mainly based on a study of the gang on the street corner (*Street Corner Society*, by William Foote Whyte, 1943) and some observations about the role of "opinions, attitudes, and beliefs (OABs)" in group behavior. My mind put together these findings and formulated one law of behavior for all social groups:

If you belong to a social group, any group, you must conform to its norms and at least pay lip service to its opinions, attitudes, and beliefs.

These things are enforced: The reward for conformity is that you will be accepted, validated, and liked by other group members. The punishment for nonconformity is that you will first be ridiculed and then be shunned or removed from the group.

The people who represent best the norms or ideals of the group have the highest status in the group. These people are allowed to deviate somewhat from absolute conformity to the norms of the group, because in their role as leaders they are allowed, even expected, to innovate. The people with the lowest status are also allowed some leeway to deviate from group norms, but only as objects of ridicule, for the amusement of other group members. The people in the middle must conform absolutely to group norms.

If a person of high status comes up with a new idea, that idea is taken seriously. If a person of low status were to come up with the same idea, that idea would be ridiculed.

All such groups are known in sociology and social psychology as "in-groups." All people who aren't a member of a particular in-group are known as the "out-group." Of course there are many social groups that are outside of any given in-group, but to the in-group they are all one out-group. All persons in the out-group have lower status than anybody in the in-group, in the opinion of in-group members.

These attitudes have been demonstrated only for small groups, such as the gang on the street corner, but I think they could also be demonstrated for large groups, such as the Catholic Church, the Hippies, and the academic community, simply by asking people what they agree with:

If you don't go to mass every week, you will burn in hell.
The mind is nothing but the physical brain.
We are all interconnected.
and so forth

I say "social laws," plural, because each group has its own set of laws to which its members must conform

We think we live in a free country, but actually we are dominated by, and must conform to, the social laws of the social groups we belong to.

The whole idea of "freedom" needs some attention. We were never free in the first place. There are natural laws and legal laws that govern our behavior. The natural laws are the laws of nature – the way things work. An example of a natural law is the law of gravity. What goes up must come down. It is possible to oppose it, but to oppose it, one must apply a greater force. These laws just exist, and govern our lives here on earth.

The legal laws are just formal versions of the social laws, for the various geographical territories we belong to. The legal laws, like all social laws, have to be enforced by human beings, with punishments ranging from a small fine to jail time and death.

So we think we live in a free country, but really we are governed by a whole network of laws. The whole idea of "freedom" in the first place was only freedom relative to the tyranny of European kings and also the priesthood. We have that relative freedom in the United States today, compared to what they do in other countries to homosexuals, women, religious heretics, and people who speak the truth.

Our Founding Fathers spoke of "inalienable rights." But if you look around the world today, you will see that human rights are not at all inalienable. Freedom of speech, freedom of religion, and freedom of sexual expression are strictly prohibited in many countries today. It should be easy to see that human rights are not God-given and inalienable, but are powers given to individuals by their governments.

In my search for a new civilization from among the "wrong" things, I immediately decided that breaking the law was not one of the "wrong" things that would lead to a new civilization. If the law had to be changed, I would try to do it legally. Actually the laws of the United States and its subdivisions have given me all the freedom I have needed to design my new civilization and present it in writing. It is the social laws of the religious, the academic, and the New Age social groups, and the culture itself, that have blocked it.

WITHDRAWAL

In 1964, as I turned 30, I was enjoying a successful career as a computer programmer, but I realized there was something more important that I wanted to do with my life, like designing a new civilization. So I withdrew from the mainstream culture to Provincetown, Massachusetts, which had been my family's summer home, ostensibly to write my philosophy, but actually to build it.

In the solitude of Cape Cod winters, I experienced what Toynbee called "withdrawal." Thoreau experienced it on the shore of Walden Pond. Isaac Newton experienced it when he moved to a family farm to escape the Plague in London and observed the falling apple.

Away from the constant cultural chatter, I was literally able to hear myself think. Instead of being constantly bombarded with other people's thoughts in books, I was more in touch with reality – sun, moon, wind, tides, migrating ducks, and my own thoughts. Removed from the cultural norms, I could see that I was becoming "strange."

Walking the sand dunes of Cape Cod, watching the irregular regularity of the ocean surf, and watching the flames in my Portland stove, I found the ideas for my new civilization.

CARL JUNG

I first read something by Carl Jung when I was 24 years old and in the Army. It seemed that he was still hung up on the spiritual beliefs of the past, while the scientific community had moved ahead to a belief in a purely physical reality. What I didn't know was that the scientific community was hung up on their belief in a purely physical universe, while Jung had moved ahead of the culture to recognize the existence of a spiritual reality, not on the basis of "faith,' and not on the "authority" of the Bible, but on the basis of EVIDENCE.

Sorry, I have to shout that word, because for 1800 years our culture has been indoctrinated into the belief that you have to believe on "faith." In fact, the Gnostics, who believed on the basis of evidence way back then, were put to death. And I suppose that believing on the basis of evidence from that time forward was branded as "heresy" and punishable by horrible torture and horrible death.

But Carl Jung saw evidence of the spiritual in the dreams of his patients. First of all, to call dreams "evidence," you have to recognize that dreams are real. Contemporary biologists of the very highest status (Francis Crick and Edward O. Wilson) have called dreams "insanity." But here we must be able to differentiate: These people have the highest qualifications in biology, but they have absolutely no qualifications in the study of dreams.

Freud called dreams "the royal road to the unconscious." He recognized that dreams were a way that the unconscious had of expressing itself. But then he called dreams "wish-fulfillment." That puts them back in fantasy-land again.

Jung improved on Freud's view by describing dreams as "a compensation for, or correction to, the conscious attitude." The "compensation" part agrees with Freud's wish-fulfillment, at least partly: If you are down in the dumps, the dreams will give you a boost. But also, if you have too high an opinion of yourself, the dreams will drop you off a cliff.

Jung's description of dreams as "correction" takes the understanding of dreams one step farther than Freud's: In order to be a "correction," dreams must be a source of truth. This of course is the exact opposite of the "insanity" of dreams as claimed by the famous biologists. But I have received an education from my dreams, which I will summarize in the next section, an education which I consider to be of equal value to my Harvard education or my four years of psychotherapy. And many many dreamworkers have done the same. Jung's description of dreams as "correction," thereby implying that they are a source of truth, has been verified many many times over.

Freud saw the unconscious only as a garbage dump for unwanted thoughts, feelings, desires, and memories. But Jung saw it also as a source of ideas and spiritual inspiration. He recognized universal dream symbols, which he called "archetypes," which came from what he called the "collective unconscious" – an unconscious base shared by all humanity in common. Again, I experienced many of these archetypes in my dream-education – the shadow, the anima, the wise old man, the great mother, and the voice. So this is not just theory; this has been verified in my own life's experience.

Jung's greatest discovery was his discovery of "original experience," the discovery that it is possible to see God for oneself. But, he warns, it can be overpowering to look upon the face of God. He tells the story of one monk who looked upon the face of God, and whose experience was so overpowering that it took him 15 years to assimilate it. And he tells of another monk who wasn't so fortunate, and just went insane.

This opened me up to the possibility that the existence of God did not have to be believed on the basis of "faith" or on the "authority" of a book that was written thousands of years ago, but could be established scientifically, on the basis of EVIDENCE.

Yes, I have to keep shouting this, because the scientists don't want to hear it. The scientific community should have recognized that Jung's discoveries were scientific at the time he wrote these things. But the scientific community was so mesmerized by the idea that all reality had to be physical and all evidence had to be evidence of the physical senses that they dismissed Jung as a "mystic."

So I had to learn about Carl Jung from a Provincetown artist, because he had hardly been mentioned in all the psychology books I had read. And in December 1966, I read *The Basic Writings of C.G. Jung*, with the help of my 9-pound dictionary. I think it also helped to read the chapters in chronological order, so that I could follow his thinking as he developed it.

I asked myself, "Where did he find his archetypes?" And the answer was that he found them in people's dreams. So I set out to explore my dreams in search of archetypes. But the dreams themselves had another purpose in mind. They were picking up where my psychiatrist had left off.

DREAM ANALYSIS

I had a little dream that told me that I was still psychologically only 10 years old, and that this was normal for the culture. There were lesbians in the dream.

This was a shock to me. I had thought, when my psychiatrist told me that I was normal and OK, and that I could end the treatment, that I had become psychologically an adult. I certainly felt much more comfortable as an adult. I was truly normal, but the little dream was telling me that that was psychological age 10. And just to prove it, there were some 10-year-old boys in real life that wanted to play with me.

I didn't realize at the time what an important discovery that was. I didn't even include the little dream in *Re-Educating Myself*. But the average person in our culture was using only the mental potential that he or she had at age 10. In *Dirty Science* I compared my discovery to Isaac Newton observing the falling apple, and a reviewer picked up on it and recognized its importance. Actually I am more like Balboa, standing on a mountain and discovering the Pacific Ocean, and recognizing that there was a whole other ocean to cross before Europeans could reach the Indies by sailing west. Similarly, the average person in our culture is only halfway to realizing his or her full adult mental potential.

Well, it was only a little dream, but then how else would you explain why 74 million people voted for Donald Trump?

I didn't mention before that there were lesbians in the dream, because I didn't want to get into the political arguments over homosexuality. But yes, at age 10, boys would rather play with boys and girls would rather play with girls, although no sex is involved. So it follows that at psychological age 10, people of the same sex would relate to each other more comfortably than with persons of the opposite sex. The homosexuals dismiss this as old-fashioned thinking and claim that homosexuality is biologically determined. They claim that homosexuals are psychologically normal, which they are, of course, because being normal is being psychologically 10 years old. I am willing to agree that there is a biological component to homosexuality, but I believe there is also a psychological component. That is why there are lesbians in the dream, representing people who are psychologically 10 years old.

I had another little dream where I was trying to go upriver on a raft. This raft had cross-pieces above the deck, so that when I had a woman aboard, the cross-pieces became submerged, and I couldn't make any progress against the current.

The message of this dream was obvious: "I can't make it with a woman." I reasoned that if I could make it to the psychological age of puberty, or psychological age 14, my sex life would improve. So, having nothing else to do all winter, I decided that I would analyze my own dreams, with that goal in mind.

I dreamed that the first 3 letters of "Superman" were "S-E-X."

I struggled with that one a while, trying to make some sense out of S = sex, U = uterus, and P = penis.

Then finally I saw it: The man who is still a boy psychologically but thinks he is a man thinks he must become Superman to achieve his goals in life, when really all he has to do is become a man.

The reference to Superman is a commentary on Nietzsche, who was psychologically 12 years old.

In 1966, interpreting one's own dreams was just not done. Only professionals were allowed to do that. But, as I have said, I had learned certain disciplines in psychotherapy. I had learned how to recognize my own defenses. I had developed some skill at interpreting dreams. And before psychotherapy, I had learned how to pour out my own honest, uninhibited thoughts with "scribbling." After psychotherapy, when I got into an emotional situation, I was able to ask myself, "How would my psychiatrist have handled this?" And I was satisfied with the results. So really, after four years of training with a psychiatrist, and 11 years total studying psychology and my own personal psychology, I was ready to be my own therapist.

And for others who may want to interpret their own dreams, I am saying that I don't think it is going to work unless you have had similar training in psychotherapy and in your own psychology. Since I have no license to practice psychotherapy, I suggest that you consult with a licensed psychotherapist before you try to interpret your own dreams. I found the key to a new civilization through dream-interpretation, but I say, "Psychotherapy is the way to a new civilization," because I believe that the disciplines I learned in psychotherapy were absolutely necessary to enable me to do that. Again, I would not expect you to be able to solve a differential equation (or even know what that is) without some knowledge of calculus.

Carl Jung added some important things to the knowledge I already had about the interpretation of dreams. First of all, as I have said, he improved upon Freud's view of dreams as "wish-fulfillment" with his view of dreams as a "compensation for, or correction to, the conscious attitude." To approach a dream, first of all, Jung would say, "I have absolutely no idea what this dream means." This is important, because dreams are telling you things you don't know. This is in contrast to things you learn in school, where you may already know part or all of what you are being taught. That is what makes dream-interpretation so hard.

Jung said that one should use one's intuition to discover what a dream means – that one should play one's hunches. Again, it was important that I had uncovered my intuition in psychotherapy, because otherwise I would not even have had this mental faculty to use.

And then, according to Jung, when one had a hunch of what a dream might mean, all of the details of the dream had to be consistent with the message of the dream. So here is the intellect checking out one's intuition.

I asked myself, "What would happen if my interpretations of my dreams are wrong? Would I just go sailing off into some La-La Land?"

The dreams themselves answered that question. I was having dreams which I interpreted as "homosexual" – fire in the corporate chimney, and dreams of the dentist, the guy who puts his tool in your mouth. I thought I might be homosexual. That wouldn't be any problem in Provincetown. So I began adjusting mentally to life as a homosexual when I had the following dream:

A beautiful woman is lying naked on a couch, drooling with desire for me. As I start towards her, suddenly I am in a car full of boys, teenagers or homosexuals, riding around town and having a wonderful time. But all I want to do is get out of that car and back to that woman. Finally, with a supreme lunge, I get out of the car – and wake up.

For a week afterward, I was trying to get back into that dream and back to that woman. I have never again thought that I might be homosexual.

And I have never again wondered what would happen if my interpretation of a dream were wrong. If your interpretation of a dream is wrong, the dreams themselves will correct you. I am switching here from the personal to the general because many other people have made the same discovery. Carl Jung mentioned it in a paper published in 1931 (although I was not aware of that until 2004). Most of the dreamworkers that I talked to at dream conferences in 1991 and 2013 were aware of it. It is simply an extension of Carl Jung's description of dreams as a correction to the conscious attitude. If the interpretation becomes part of the conscious attitude, the dreams can correct it.

This correction process I call "The Self-Steering Process." It functions like the self-steering mechanisms on ocean-going yachts that keep them on course. The farther off course they are, the stronger the pull to bring them back on course. With such a self-steering process steering us towards the truth, dream analysis can be more accurate than conscious thinking.

Except for taking two weeks off for Christmas and New Year's, I devoted my entire winter of 1966 and 1967 to analyzing my own dreams, 24/7, dreaming by night and analyzing by day. It was the greatest wisdom I have ever experienced. When I really paid attention to my dreams, the theatre of the unconscious put on some truly great performances, and they were all tailored specifically to my educational needs. I'll say it again: I compare this 3-month period of dream analysis as equal in educational value to my Harvard education or my four years of psychotherapy.

I produced, in this period, 880 pages of dreams, analyses, scribbling, and other writing. I did not write down all the thoughts that were racing through my head during that period. I boiled down the experience to a meaningful 40 pages in *Re-Educating Myself.* I am not going to include that detail here, first of all because this is a summary, and second because this is my dream experience, tailored to my specific educational needs, and your dream experience would be different.

In summary, my dreams took me to places that my psychiatrist had missed. He was truly the best that the culture could provide, but he didn't believe in the spiritual, and he missed my most serious traumatic experience, from age 2 1/2. Also, of course, becoming normal was the goal of psychotherapy. Nobody in the profession knew that being normal was being psychologically 10 years old and that there was farther to go to reach psychological adulthood.

In order to reach the psychological age of puberty, I had to resolve that major traumatic experience from my childhood, and in order to resolve that trauma, I had to become a spiritual person and forgive the man who traumatized me. The awareness, acceptance, and assimilation of the spiritual had to come first.

The dreams handled all this wonderfully. They started off with combat lessons, appropriately for a 10-year-old boy, dealing with wild predatory animals in the wilderness – bears, lions, and wolves. A reptile came up out of a swimming pool and was on me in a second. I was killed many times. But I was learning how to defend myself.

And then there was the dream of the white wolf:

The white wolf was coming to me, nuzzling, as a friendly dog might come. But still it was a wolf and it could kill me. There were wildcats in the dream, and I told it, "Go chase that cat!" And off it went and chased the cats away. Then it came back again in a friendly way. But this was an animal to be feared, so I started choking it, but then I realized that all its claws were facing me and it could rip me to pieces.

This was my first lesson in the spiritual: Here was an animal that could kill me for food but didn't seem to want to.

At about that time I read a biography of Marco Polo, who traveled as a teenager with his father to the court of the Khan. He showed no fear of the Khan, while most people would grovel and quake in the presence of the Khan, who could put to death anybody that displeased him. And this amused the Khan, that this young man should have absolutely no fear of him.

And why should this amuse the Khan? Why shouldn't he just think this young man stupid for not recognizing that he had the power to kill him? Obviously there was some other value than sheer physical power operating here.

My dreams introduced the spiritual to me in business transactions, too, such as giving a waiter a tip. There is an element of trust here. The tip is not required, and it is paid after the service is performed, so it has no effect on the service being performed, but it certainly creates good feelings from the waiter towards you.

Gradually, various spiritual values worked their way into my dreams. The bull moose became the symbol of my masculinity – "the moose principle," as I called it. The bull moose in the dream didn't attack. But he didn't run away, either. This symbol of strength without aggression was perfect for me.

Hunters think the moose is stupid, because he will just stand there and let himself be shot.

Finally, the dreams came right out and announced the spiritual, with a dream about a great ship, half buried in the sand, with 5 out of 7 masts still intact, being resurrected and sailing over land and sea, being saluted by guards waking from their slumber. This was my spiritual self, finally being awakened from its slumber.

The ship steered an 'S' course in the water, clearly indicating "spirit" or "soul." It was going out of Provincetown Harbor on a course that would take it into Provincetown Harbor. And a cold wind blew from the south, not the north. I learned that dreams which showed the opposite of physical reality were spiritual dreams.

Light, in my dreams, was a symbol of love. In one dream, I was in the dark and brushed up against a lion. Instead of being afraid, I said, "Oh, you poor thing, all alone in the dark." And immediately the sun came out and we were no longer in the dark.

This was modeled on an actual experience of a woman I knew who was trying to get to my door past 3 large dogs, lunging at their chains. Instead of being afraid, she showed compassion for them and said, "Oh, you poor things, all chained up." And they settled down and let her pass.

This was a lesson in compassion. Real love is compassion, caring about the other guy. The Beatles sang, "All you need is love."

But what is love? There are many meanings of "love." Love is something you fall in. "Love" is a word that is used to manipulate you, as in "I love you; therefore you are obliged to love me." Love is passion, as in "I love ice cream" or "I love sex." But as one moves into psychological maturity, love also includes compassion for all beings, including oneself.

I dreamed of a light more powerful than the sun shining through a fog bank, and in front of the fog bank a small gold cross.

I interpreted this to mean that this powerful Light was Love, which was the supreme power of the universe. This was an affirmation of "GOD IS LOVE," that I had seen as a child on the wall of the Christian Science Church. This was the proof of my hypothesis, "I will believe in God when I see God." The dream even announced that this was an "original experience."

But this wasn't the God of the Judeo/Christian tradition, with all the attributes that had been laid on their God. All I knew was that God was the Light, which was Love, which was the supreme power of the universe.

And the small gold cross, of course, was Christ, who "makes intercession for us."

If this interpretation was wrong, it would have been corrected by the self-steering process, but it has never been corrected.

It was necessary for me to have compassion in order to resolve my traumatic experience from age 2 1/2. I had been left with a babysitter I liked, and a man I didn't like came to visit her. I must have bugged him in some way, because he attacked me with words I didn't understand, like (making this up) "little rich son of a bitch," indicating that he was of a different social class, which also I didn't understand. All I understood was that it had something to do with my father's social position. I decided that my father must have done something awful to this man to make him so angry. So I decided that I didn't want to grow up to be like my father.

When my mother came home, she was cold to me. So I decided that my mother didn't love me any more.

My psychiatrist said, "Well, they probably just told her you were a very bad boy." We didn't pursue it any further. And we probably couldn't have, until I acquired the spiritual quality of compassion.

I grew up with vengeance on my mind, thinking "Some day I'll be big and strong, and then I'll show him." I took on all the bullies, because that was my problem.

So now, at age 32, as the problem unraveled itself, I thought, "He must be 70 by now. I can find him and beat the shit out of him."

And then I realized he was just a poor unfortunate, angered by the inequalities of life, and probably out of work, because all of this happened in the daytime. And I felt compassion for him. I forgave him for taking out his anger upon me, because actually he had to suffer from it all his life. (The dreams helped me with this, too, by dramatizing the suffering of the lower classes.) This resolved the traumatic experience.

Having acquired compassion, and having cleared myself of the desire for revenge, I was ready for the psychological age of puberty:

It is my first day in the Coast Guard. I am out in the dunes, in the wilderness, eating my lunch which is leftovers from breakfast – half an orange, half a grapefruit, and some scraps. I eat the half-orange and save the rest. Somebody comes along, and I offer to share my lunch with him, but I hide the grapefruit and offer him only the scraps. He doesn't want any.

Then I start walking up over a dune and confront a moose. The moose doesn't run or attack, but just stands there. Then there is a scene with a bear chasing me. I run around a tree, confusing him, and get away.

I am standing on the dune in front of Race Point Coast Guard Station. The waves are getting big. A man stands fishing on the beach, his little boy standing on the palm of his hand, his wife sitting beside him. He puts the boy down as he fixes his line, and the boy runs close to the surf, which threatens to sweep him away. He hollers to his wife to watch the kid. My attention is diverted as she yells something about the strength of the undertow and her helplessness.

Now the tide comes in, covering most of the sand bank. Something like a knife splashes in the water. I look closer and see 14-foot man-eating sharks come in, and I swim (now in three feet of water) for the high ground.

A call has come in for the Coast Guard to rescue man, woman, and child under 120 feet of water. My job is to go out in a tiny aluminum boat and mark the spot. The blackness of the deep water is terrifying. The sharks will surely capsize the boat and rip my belly out. It is certain death, but as the junior member, I must go to sea in this tiny boat. There are bigger boats, but I haven't earned the right to use them.

Two men are standing, holding the boat for me. I realize that in joining the service I have volunteered to die if necessary, but I can't stand the idea that this is my very last day, when suddenly I have so much to live for – this was to be my wedding day. But this is my job – I can't hesitate now. As I step into the boat, I wake up with a jolt.

I was never so glad to be alive as I was after that dream. The day seemed sunnier, and the colors seemed brighter, than ever before.

In the morning of the dream, I was unwilling to share half a grapefruit, but in the afternoon I was willing to give my life for man, woman, and child.

The number 14 indicated that this was psychological age 14. This was the psychological age of puberty. This was an important transition point where my "human nature" itself changed, from the exclusive self-interest of the child to an equally natural motivation to give and share and even sacrifice myself for others, as is more appropriate for an adult with children of one's own.

I say "my" human nature changed, because some people deny that children are greedy and selfish. Some children may in fact have high spiritual values in place. But I think the normal child is motivated purely by his or her self-interest. That is nature's way for survival of the species, that the child, who is weaker than the adult and more vulnerable, should be dedicated exclusively to his or her own self-interest in order to maximize his or her survival potential. That translates to greed and selfishness.

The other half of the equation is that survival of the species is not only survival of the fittest. It is survival of the greatest number. That is accomplished sometimes by the one sacrificing oneself for the many.

Certainly, the American system of competitive self-interest, which is based on greed and selfishness, seems to work better than more altruistic systems, like socialism. I am saying that this is because the American system is better suited to the psychology of the normal person, who is psychologically 10 years old.

I estimate that 5% of Americans have reached this level of compassion and altruism at the psychological age of puberty. If a majority were to reach it, they would elect a different kind of leaders, and we would have a whole new level of civilization.

Actually, I lied when I said "new civilization." I was just being polite. What we really have now is a semi-barbarous system: "Thou shalt not kill, except when your country orders you to kill." Before we can truly call ourselves "civilized," major nations have to end the practice of warfare and have to keep minor nations under control.

And yes, my sex life improved, but actually it improved at every step of the way through psychotherapy and continued to improve as I developed further to psychological adulthood. It is interesting that my selfish desire for sexual pleasure led me to a state of unselfishness which helped me to fulfill my selfish desire for sexual pleasure.

As I write this now, my solution for world peace and the survival of the human species, 56 years after its discovery, I have to stop and discuss some of the ways people have denied my discovery.

Some have just argued that human nature is human nature and cannot be changed.

But I think the most prevalent argument is that we have always known compassion and altruism, and that I have discovered nothing new.

Yes, a few people, 5% by my estimate, are genuinely compassionate and altruistic, but others know that compassion and altruism are good things to have, so they fake it. They play a role, like actors in a movie, just as I played a role when I was psychologically 4 years old. But it is one thing to play the role of Joan of Arc in a movie, and something else to actually be that person.

What I am talking about starts with the discovery of a real self. Many of us abandon that real self at an early age. We are asked to share our toys with other children. We don't want to share our toys. So we see that we are inferior to what the adults want us to be, and what will win their approval. So we abandon our real self in favor of an artificial self that will get the approval of adults.

That real self has to be discovered and raised to maturity. That real self matured psychologically will be motivated by compassion and altruism to the depth of one's being. This was my discovery.

So I offer you the test that I gave to myself: At what age did you like yourself the best? If you can immediately spot some childhood age, then that is most likely your real self, or some important aspect of it, which you abandoned at that age. It is only that real self, and not any artificial self, that can reach the psychological age of puberty.

We have this thing called "morality." Morality is simply behaving as a psychologically mature person would behave. Morality is forced on young children before they are psychologically ready to behave that way. It would be better to let children be children and let them grow naturally into "moral" behavior. That way they would be less likely to abandon their real selves.

In *Re-Educating Myself*, I talked about "moral laws." But moral laws are just social laws coming from religion and enforced by people. Yes, they are based on what people think it must be like to attain psychological maturity. But not all these people have attained psychological maturity, so it is only what these people imagine it is, and they could be wrong.

Dream analysis is more in the realm of natural law. Dreams are a natural function of human beings. With the self-steering process, dreams will even go so far as to correct your interpretation of them, like a teacher correcting your homework. So, if you can learn the language of dreams and pick up on the hints they are giving you, you can get an education from dreams.

But please note that this is not an authoritarian education, such as what you had in school. First of all, you never have to do this. You can simply assume that "dreams are a random firing of neurons" and go merrily on your way, paying them no attention. Or you can assume that dreams are "insanity," oblivious of the hint that the dreams are trying to tell you about YOUR insanity. And the second reason why dreams are not authoritarian is because they usually communicate with only hints of the truth and symbols. You have to figure out what these hints and symbols mean. You have to interpret the dream with your rational faculties, in order to make any sense out of it. And many times you have to be able to overcome your psychological defenses in order to understand the meaning of a dream. The dreams aren't doing that for you. You have to do that for yourself with your rational faculties.

We have religion, which is an authoritarian system telling us what to believe, and "spirituality," which is other people setting themselves up as so-called "authorities" and telling us what to believe. Dream analysis is a natural alternative to both of these systems and does not depend on any external "authorities" to tell us what to believe. Our own rational abilities tell us what to believe. We study our dreams with our rational abilities just as scientists study the natural environment. It looks like chaos to start with, but then as scientists formulate "laws" of nature, it makes more sense. The same is true of dreams. The dreams are nature, trying to tell us what is true, not in an authoritarian way, but only hinting at it, so that we have to figure it out ourselves, from apparent chaos. And what my dreams told me was that the spiritual is real.

In *Re-Educating Myself*, I said that I know that the spiritual is real because the same process that resolved my traumatic experience and changed my "human nature" also told me that the spiritual was real. Now I am saying that I would not have had the compassion, the altruism, and the forgiveness to have accomplished these things if the spiritual had not already become an important part of my life. The spiritual comes first. The awareness, the acceptance, and the assimilation of the spiritual are absolutely necessary in order to reach the psychological age of puberty. I am switching now from the particular to the general because I am dealing here with abstractions: Compassion and altruism are spiritual qualities.

It is important to differentiate between the spiritual and religion. "Religion" I have defined as a way of approaching and dealing with the spiritual. The spiritual is the reality. Religion is only a system created by people to deal with that reality. Dream analysis, for me, has been my way of approaching the spiritual. I am not saying that dream analysis is a new religion. Dream analysis is not a religion. I am only saying that dream analysis is a better way, a more natural way, of approaching the spiritual than religion. My behavior is "moral," not because somebody is forcing me to be this way, but because I WANT to be this way.

David Elkins, in *Beyond Religion*, describes 8 ways of approaching the spiritual outside of religion.

Approaching the spiritual is fine, but dealing with it is something else. Religion has helped people to deal with the spiritual. Carl Jung said that the dogma of the Catholic Church helped to protect people from the dangers of original experience. I experienced this in the dream where I saw the Light. Tada was in that dream. I knew that she was dead, and that was frightening, so I crossed myself. We both crossed ourselves, although neither of us were Catholic. It just seemed to take away the fear.

So I had experienced the spiritual, but I had to learn how to deal with it. I was in the same position as the Hippies, although they had blasted themselves off into inner space with psychedelic drugs, whereas my introductory trip into the spiritual, as I dreamed it, was a leisurely sailing trip down through the islands.

I said, in *Re-Educating Myself*, "It is one thing to search for the truth, and something else to bring it back alive." I didn't realize until just now (2023) that by moving outside the culture, I was in everybody's out-group, according to the social laws.

I think of myself as an explorer of the mental. I compare myself to Balboa, standing on a mountain and discovering that there was a whole other ocean to cross before Europeans could reach the Indies by sailing west. Wasn't he only one person making that discovery? No, he wasn't. He had a retinue of more than a thousand men, to protect him from the native Americans. He had status in the culture. All he had to do was write a letter to the King of Spain, and his discovery was official.

And who am I? Who authorized me to set out on my journey of exploration? Could I have just written a letter to President Johnson to make my discovery official?

According to the social laws, which I recognize, only persons with the highest status in the social group are allowed to make innovations. Only important people are allowed to say important things. Unimportant people who claim to be saying important things are viewed as arrogant, and ridiculed.

But the discoveries of unimportant people are sometimes recognized by important people, as was the case when the young mathematician John Couch Adams calculated the position of Neptune before it was actually observed by astronomers, and was given a letter of introduction to the Astronomer Royal.

So I am hoping for that kind of support from important people, and have received some already. I am hoping you can set aside the opinions, attitudes, and beliefs of your social group while you are reading this book, and just look at it with your natural intelligence.

This will not be so easy, because psychologists no longer study the mind, and all academic people have been biased against studying their own minds through psychotherapy.

I am wondering how many discoveries made by unimportant people were not recognized by important people, and lost to the culture as a result?

BEYOND PSYCHOLOGY

Once my childhood traumatic experiences were resolved, I began having strange dreams that I didn't know how to interpret, until I had the following dream:

Movie camera car, taking pictures, coming to railroad crossing, almost colliding with huge locomotive coming on tracks at an oblique angle. Car doesn't stop, just keeps going, approaching intersection as light turns yellow, red, then instantly green as camera car goes through. I remember having seen this before, look in rear-view mirror of camera car and see my '48 Olds following behind. I am trying to get a better look to see if it is really me.

This camera car that always travels at a constant rate of speed represents the passage of time. And if I am seeing my '48 Olds in the rear-view mirror, then what I am seeing in front is the future. Once I had resolved my issues of the past, I began dreaming of the future.

The problem of dreaming of the future is that I never know what the dream means until the thing actually happens. I dreamed I had a confrontation with the police on a side street and then actually got a parking ticket on a side street. I dreamed that I pulled way over to the right to avoid being hit by a car that didn't seem to want to change lanes to pass me, and then found myself in exactly the same situation. Then I dreamed that a huge wave hit Provincetown. This was also a dream of the future, but it was symbolic. The huge wave was the Hippies, and their takeover of the culture was very painful to me.

I dreamed that I was having a good time with a friend that I hadn't seen for more than a year. He showed up the next day. I told him about the dream, and he argued that it didn't have to be a dream of the future. It could have been telepathic, because he had been planning this trip for a while.

And so, many apparently precognitive dreams might be inter-
preted as being telepathic, if they reflect what people have on their
minds, such as the 9/11 attacks.

But a little more than a year after this visit from my friend, in
December 1968, when I was living on Beacon Hill in Boston, I had
the following dream:

> *It was a cold morning as I started off to work. My car was parked on the
> left-hand side of the street. I left the door open as I got in to start it. I turned
> the key in the ignition and nothing happened. It wouldn't start.*

About an hour later, I started off to work. It was a cold morning.
My car was parked on the left-hand side of the street. I left the
door open as I got in to start it. As I put the key in the ignition, I
remembered the dream. "Foolishness!" I thought. My car had
never failed to start in the five years I had owned it. So I confi-
dently turned the key. And nothing happened. It wouldn't start.
There was a subtle problem in the starter wiring that was finally
solved by an expert mechanic after 5 trips to 3 different garages.

So here was a dream of a condition known only to a mindless
piece of machinery – clearly a dream of the future and not a result
of telepathy.

Somewhere along in here, I discovered the "mental senses."
They are described in my 1970 manuscript.

In order to understand a proposition such as "If $\underline{A}$ is greater
than $\underline{B}$, and $\underline{B}$ is greater than $\underline{C}$, then $\underline{A}$ is greater than $\underline{C}$," I don't
compare the letters on the paper. I construct some kind of images
in my mind and then compare those images. In order to compare
these things, I must be able to perceive something in my mind.
When somebody explains something to me and I say, "I see," I am
not seeing with my eyes, but I am perceiving something in my
mind. The mechanisms by which we perceive the contents of our
minds and our mental processes – thoughts, emotions, memories,
and dreams – I call the "mental senses." All normal people have
these mental senses.

But our culture traditionally has recognized the 5 physical
senses and then uses the expression "sixth sense" to describe some
kind of psychic ability. So the culture knows nothing about these
mental senses.

When I remember a face, I am using the mental senses. When I experience a dream, I am using my mental senses. When I remember the dream, I am using other mental senses. When I am feeling emotion, I am using mental senses. Now that I am hard of hearing, I can actually play back from memory the exact recording of what a person said, if I didn't get it the first time.

Descartes mistrusted the senses, and this led him to proclaim, "I think; therefore I am. (*Cogito ergo sum.*)" But how did he know he was thinking, unless he first sensed it?

I had been introduced to the spiritual. I wanted to know more about it. In June 1967, soon after my dream winter, an old girlfriend came to Provincetown and handed me a copy of *There Is a River: The Story of Edgar Cayce*, by Thomas Sugrue.

Edgar Cayce (pronounced "Casey") could put himself into a trance state and access information that he was not consciously aware of. At these "readings," as they were called, there was always a conductor asking the questions and a stenographer recording everything that was said. Most of the readings (more than 9000) were medical readings, diagnosing people's illnesses and prescribing a cure. He always worked with medical doctors, who wrote the necessary prescriptions. In more than 9000 medical readings, many of them cases where conventional medicine had failed, he was proven right more than 90% of the time. Follow-up correspondence, along with the readings themselves, is on file at the Association for Research and Enlightenment (A.R.E.) in Virginia Beach, and available for examination by qualified researchers.

He also did more than 2500 "life readings," describing people's past incarnations and their effect on those people's present lives. The life readings, of course, could not be verified, but I saw them as proof of reincarnation.

Here was a process that was proven right in 90% of 9000 medical readings. So the probability of the process being right can be taken as 90%, and the probability of it being wrong, in any one life reading, was 10%. So then the probability of it being wrong, in every one of 2500 life readings, in asserting that reincarnation was a fact, was 10^{-2500}, a number so small that it might as well be zero.

What made it more convincing was that the conscious Edgar Cayce did not believe in reincarnation. He was a devout Christian, who read the Bible once for every year of his life. And the Bible made no mention of reincarnation.

He struggled with this. He said, "If this is wrong, I don't want to do it." But then, he couldn't find anything in the Bible against reincarnation, either. Eventually he found passages in the Bible that suggested reincarnation:

John 8:58 ... Before Abraham was, I am.

John 9:2 ... Who did sin, this man, or his parents, that he was born blind?

Nobody put the idea of reincarnation into his head. He came out with it himself. A man named Arthur Lammers asked him for a horoscope, and Cayce said that in a previous incarnation the man had been a monk.

Evil forces sometimes give us truth so that we will believe their lies. Was Edgar Cayce a pawn of these evil forces, giving people truth in the medical readings and lies in the life readings?

The best argument I can give against that is that Edgar Cayce was not a medium. He did not communicate with spirit entities. All his readings came from his own perceptions, from "God's book of remembrances," as he called it. He visualized the experience as going into a huge library with huge books. This was identified in the books I read about Cayce as the Akashic Records. There is a record in the universe of everything that has ever happened, if you just know how to access it. The exact same process that was accessing information for the medical readings was accessing it for the life readings.

Along with reincarnation is the Law of Karma. This is the other half of the Golden Rule, "Do unto others as you would have them do unto you." Because whatever you do unto others will be done unto you. Those that live by the sword shall die by the sword, if not in this incarnation, then in another, or several.

One of the Beatles described reincarnation as "You have to keep coming back until you get it right." It seemed to me that this was similar to psychological problems in this lifetime. You have to keep repeating the same situation until you get it right. You don't have to believe in reincarnation to see the Law of Karma in action.

I was inclined to believe Edgar Cayce because he knew things about psychology that I knew but that the professionals in the field did not know. So I was ready to accept, at least as working hypotheses, the things he said on wild subjects such as Atlantis or levitation. I mean, how would the ancients have moved bluestones weighing 2 to 4 tons to Stonehenge across water, marsh, and dry land?

The academic community, on the other hand, has treated Edgar Cayce with ignorance, with prejudice, and with slander. They have whispered that he was a fraud, without any evidence to back it up.

Actually, two academic people investigated Cayce. The first was Hugo Munsterberg of Harvard in 1912. He came to expose Cayce, and left saying that the case warranted more study. He never came back. He was the victim of prejudice against Germans in World War I, and died in 1916.

The second was William Moseley Brown of Washington and Lee in 1928. After a thorough investigation, he said, "I can't expose it. Still, it's not the sort of thing you can do nothing about. I can't ignore it. I'll have to believe in it."

If academic people know of any studies which would demonstrate that Edgar Cayce was in any way fraudulent, they need to come forward with this evidence, because they have lost credibility with their opinion of Cayce.

Or maybe they are just being stupid. They hold the belief, "Psychic abilities don't exist." Here is evidence that psychic abilities do exist, and they throw away the evidence in order to protect their ignorance.

Edgar Cayce made prophecies that were wrong about cataclysmic earth changes that were to occur at the end of the twentieth century. But he always emphasized that future events, even earth changes, depended on the free will of human beings. If you take everything Edgar Cayce said as a working hypothesis, as I do, you should have no trouble with his errors.

The Hippies distorted what Edgar Cayce was saying. Cayce said, "You are what you eat and what you think." The Hippies truncated that to "You are what you eat." Cayce said in many readings, "Mind is the builder." The Hippies totally distorted that in the advertising of the A.R.E. Press. The Hippies just had to get rid of the mind.

In the summer of 1967, I dreamed of a woman with black lips — the kiss of death. I had a girlfriend that introduced me to marijuana.

I didn't dare take LSD. My dreams had shown me that it could make me crazy to open myself up to truths before I was psychologically ready to accept them. But marijuana seemed mild, and at least it seemed that it would give me some idea of what the drug experience was all about.

The marijuana made my girlfriend into the most beautiful woman in the world, which she wasn't. We did a lot of giggling. All that was nice.

But then dead people started coming into my dreams. The first was a woman I had liked, who had died when I was 7. But when I looked into the blackness of her eyes, I was terrified.

The dreams progressed to real heavies, like something out of a horror movie. I dreamed that the phone rang and it was the dead on the line. I hung up the phone, but it just kept on talking.

Then I had a dream that told me, "Marijuana is poison." I never smoked marijuana again, or ever even wanted to breathe it.

For about a year after smoking marijuana, I always knew exactly when the traffic light was going to turn green. But that was a small advantage in life, for the price I had to pay for it.

Now that marijuana is being made legal, I want to repeat my message for the benefit of all those innocent people who will think it is perfectly OK to smoke it, FDA approved. Marijuana is poison. It will open you up to things you aren't psychologically ready to deal with.

I went to a psychiatrist to deal with the problem of the dead people coming into my dreams. He was highly recommended by two different people. But he didn't believe there was such a thing as dead people coming into my dreams. He just thought I had a deep-seated problem. I realized I was beyond the help of the psychiatric profession. I was on my own.

Edgar Cayce had taught me that living human beings had all the attributes that spirit entities had, plus a human body. I had a will, and a simple act of will was enough to keep the spirit entities out of my environment. That was OK for a start, but it was hard work.

With the marijuana, I was carried away, night after night, in spiritual dreams, so that I began to wonder whether I was still sane.

At this point I met a spiritual teacher. She helped to calm me down. She taught me how to meditate, and when I meditated, I saw clouds. She told me I could expect to see more clearly if my body were not clouded by those carnal things – meat and sex and coffee and cigarettes. This experience inspired the following dream:

A spiritual teacher was lecturing me on the laws of the real universe. First she pointed out the physical laws, quite clearly, just as I understand them: sex and reproduction, kill to eat, kill to survive – the laws of the jungle. Those were the <u>first</u> level laws. Then, from the jungle scene, we passed over some clouds – things were kind of vague – until we reached another clear scene. This, she said, was the <u>third</u> level, and she very clearly explained the laws on this third level. I don't remember what they were, except that they were spiritual laws and they were as clear and valid as the physical laws.

Then the scene shifted. A toad had hopped out of his hole to see the sun or moon. There was a beautiful orange and purple sky. Then a creature the size of an eagle swooped down from the sky – eagle's wings, the face of a black leopard, and four legs – and stood over the toad. "If the toad doesn't freeze with fear," I thought to myself, "it is only one hop back to his hole: If the eagle pounces, the toad can hop, and make it."

Then, abruptly, I was the toad, looking up at this huge creature standing over me. By the physical laws, I was in danger, but this was the spiritual realm, and I wasn't so sure. At any rate it was only one hop to safety if the creature made a move. But it just stood there, with great dignity, like the Sphinx. I looked up at the face, studying the jaws and teeth. It was not a bestial face, or a frightening face, but had some spiritual quality about it – no carnal desires.

That's about as far as I have ventured into the spiritual reality – as the toad one hop from its hole. Although the second part of the dream is more dramatic, the first part was more important to me.

The traditional "spiritual" path has been to renounce the physical – certain physical appetites such as meat and sex – in favor of spiritual desires. But it was clear from this dream that <u>both</u> sets of laws, the physical and the spiritual, were precisely determined down to the last detail, and equally binding, despite their apparent inconsistencies. The spiritual path was not something that could be followed at the expense of the physical, but the human being, as a complete entity, was subject to both. The challenge, or even the purpose, of incarnating as a physical being was to learn to reconcile the two – not to renounce one in favor of the other. My body was designed with appetites for meat and sex, and emotions like anger. It seemed that my spiritual purpose on earth was not served by <u>repressing</u> those physical drives, but by incorporating them into appropriate behavior, consistent with both the physical and the spiritual laws.

If the physical laws were the <u>first</u> level and the spiritual laws were the <u>third</u> level, then what was the <u>second</u> level? We had passed over a vague and cloudy area. That must have been the second level, but why wasn't it explained like the others?

The clouds were the clouds I had seen while meditating, the fog bank that had protected me from seeing God – the clouds of my own mind. The second level was mental. The mind is the bridge between the physical and the spiritual – the means by which we reconcile the two.

I decided to go back to computer programming, to see if I was still sane. On the first day of work, after spending about 2 hours reading the 250-page set of specifications of the project I was to be working on, I declared, "There's a major flaw in your system." Nine months later, when the project was completed as specified, I was proven right. I was still sane.

Even so, it took a couple of years for the effects of the marijuana to wear off.

I had read somewhere that some people had heart attacks because they actually willed themselves to die. With my compassion and altruism, I was so far removed from a culture that functioned on competitive self-interest, an adversarial legal system, and warfare that I was afraid I might will myself to die. The spooky dead people in my dreams made it worse, as if they were calling me to join them. For a couple of years, I was afraid to go to sleep at night, for fear that I might die.

In the spring of 1969, I was assembling the material to write my book. As I worked on this for a month or so, I realized what an enormous project I had ahead of me. Exhausted and depressed, I flopped down on my bed. I didn't care whether I lived or died.

Immediately I lost consciousness. Immediately I shot upwards out of my basement apartment at a tremendous rate of speed – up, up, up an enormous distance, into the presence of a blinding Light. I knew it was dangerous to look upon the face of God, so I shielded my eyes from the Light with my right arm. Off to my left, or the right hand of God, stood the figure of Christ. He said, very simply, "Get back to work." And back down I went, as fast as I had come up.

Then I was on a train, traveling through the night, slowing down as it approached the city. I thought I had died and was being reincarnated, and I told myself, "This time I'm not going to start smoking."

I was surprised and relieved to wake up and find myself still in the same body, in the same bed. After almost two years of living in intense fear of dying, I had finally let myself go, and found out the answer. First of all, I felt that I had experienced what it was like to die. It wasn't frightening or painful at all – just the release of the spirit to another realm. Second, the Higher Authorities weren't going to let me do anything so foolish as to will myself to die, until my time had come. I have never again been afraid of dying.

Also, from that time on, there has never been any question in my mind of whether I belonged here on earth. The word of Christ had assured me that I had work to do here – whatever that work might be. Also I felt that my work was supported by the Higher Authorities – that I was on "God's payroll."

That summer, one beautiful sunny day, I took a long walk on the dunes, and came back into town full of good thoughts and feelings. I spotted a beautiful woman with a friend of mine, and of course I was interested in meeting her.

"You are very disturbed," she said.

"What do you mean, I'm disturbed? How do you know that?"

"I just feel it," she said. "You are very disturbed."

And I <u>was</u> very disturbed. I had felt fine until she had told me I was disturbed, but now the more I argued with her, the more disturbed I became. By the time we finished talking, the sky had clouded over and it wasn't a nice day any more.

She wrote me a long letter from New York, telling me how much I needed her help. But I could see, from her negative and pessimistic outlook on life, that she had serious psychological problems herself.

I believed in God. Now, I realized, I also had to believe in Satan. Now that I was one of the least of God's employees, here was one of the least of Satan's employees, coming to mess me up.

I spent nine months organizing my book, and six months writing it. It was rejected by four publishers, and by a dominant youth culture that rejected logic, psychotherapy, and anyone over 30. I had a computer project to make ends meet, and in the winter of 1971, I was giving a course in dream analysis, as part of the Free University of Provincetown.

I was having dinner one night with a young couple, Dan and Diane, who were my two best students. I was suggesting that we put a notice in the Free U. newsletter – "MEETING TO ORGANIZE A NEW CIVILIZATION, time, place, etc."

Dan said, "Why do that? Somebody has done it already." And he handed me a paperback book, *The Ultimate Frontier*, by Eklal Kueshana – the organizational philosophy of The Stelle Group.

I realized the enormous problems involved in organizing a new civilization – just getting anyone to <u>agree</u> on anything. It seemed it would be much easier if somebody already had a nucleus of ideas to build upon. So I took the book home with me that night, and started to read.

Eklal Kueshana is the pen name of Richard Kieninger, who was educated by the Brotherhoods to lead the Nation of God at the end of this century. The Brotherhoods are secret religious organizations that have existed throughout history. *The Ultimate Frontier* is packed with information on the spiritual reality that they taught to Richard.

I had heard of the Brotherhoods. I had heard that the Masons were once really masons, who built the great cathedrals of Europe. They built them as directed by the Catholic Church, of course, but at the same time managed to incorporate into them their own religious symbolism. I had heard that the Sufi were another such secret society, operating in the Middle East around the thirteenth century – that *The Rubaiyat of Omar Khayyam* was written by a Sufi poet, and was all religious symbolism. So I was prepared to accept the existence of the Brotherhoods.

The Brotherhoods are made up of the most advanced human souls – Masters, Adepts, and other spiritually-evolved people, both male and female. They have kept their identity secret to protect themselves from persecution and death at the hands of the ruling authorities, both church and state.

One of the prerequisites for membership in the Brotherhoods is a controlled clairvoyance. I could see how it would be embarrassing to the earthly powers to have people around who could read their every thought. I could also see that clairvoyance gave the Brotherhoods a perfect system of organization. There was no need for secret handshakes or code-words. They could identify each other and communicate using senses that normal people hadn't developed.

I was fascinated to see what the Brotherhoods had to say. I read until I could read no longer. I fell asleep with the book in my lap at 4 AM, and had the following dream:

I was starting a sailboat race, but I didn't even have my sails up, and the other boats were all sailing by me. With the help of my crew, one male, one female, I got my sails up and began to move. The bow of the boat was not symmetrical, but was lopsided, like a right shoe. This somehow enabled me to sail straight for the windward mark, while the other boats had to go way off in another direction and then tack back. When I rounded the mark, none of the other boats were even in sight. I hadn't expected to be so far ahead, and I didn't know where the next mark was. There was a committee boat there, overseeing the race, and I asked the race committee for a map of the course. One of the committee members said that they didn't have an extra one, but he would let me take his. And I sailed off, into a vast, calm, white ocean that had no horizon.

The meaning of the dream was clear. It was the story of my life, up to that point. After floundering around in my college days, I had gotten off on the right foot and gone straight to my goal (developing my own potential), so that there was no longer any competition or any question of competition, but there was nobody to follow, either. I didn't know where to go from there. The race committee were the Masters of the Brotherhoods I had been reading about. The map was their philosophy, as outlined in *The Ultimate Frontier*. It was the map which would guide me on the next leg of my journey.

I read almost every word that emanated from The Stelle Group and Richard Kieninger, based on his contacts with the Brotherhoods. That information has helped me to clarify and crystallize my own thinking. To begin with, as I have said, I have taken the distinction between "information" and "knowledge" from the Brotherhoods. I shared with Richard the expression "emotional maturity," which we both changed to "psychological maturity" at about the same time.

When I visited The Stelle Group in 1971, I asked Richard what he thought of dream analysis. He said "It's ambiguous." That helped me to understand the importance of my discovery of the self-steering process, which made it unambiguous.

An important part of the Brotherhoods' teaching was the Twelve Great Virtues. They were all part of my philosophy in 1970, although I didn't identify them as such, and I certainly don't claim to have mastered them. They are defined as follows:

SINCERITY is total honesty with myself and with others.

KINDNESS means never to hurt another person. I have had trouble reconciling sincerity and kindness, and have decided that sincerity is kindness, even if it is unpleasant. Of course it can be expressed in the kindest possible way.

PRECISION means to strive for the highest degree of accuracy, both in understanding things and expressing myself.

EFFICIENCY means not to waste my time on earth, but to use it efficiently, to the best of my abilities.

HUMILITY means knowing exactly where I stand. It does not mean false humility, or self-deprecation. For example, Muhammad Ali, when he said "I'm the greatest," was expressing humility.

COURAGE doesn't mean lack of fear. It means pursuing my objectives in the face of fear.

TOLERANCE means recognizing that if I were that other person in that particular situation, I would be doing exactly the same thing.

FORBEARANCE is the same as tolerance, in those cases where I am actually injured by another person. It means forgiveness, and no desire for retaliation.

DEVOTION means dedication to a task or a purpose.

CHARITY means giving to others in need, but only if they ask for it.

PATIENCE is the willingness to wait for the outworking of natural processes, as in psychological growth.

DISCERNMENT is differentiation, or knowing the difference, taken to the highest level.

It is also interesting to note the "virtues" that are not on the list, such as obedience, chastity, and vegetarian diet.

The Brotherhoods advocate a natural growth process, without any artificial methods or restraints, or any submission to "authorities." Learning to practice the Virtues in one's daily life, they say, is the foundation for spiritual growth. In my experience, the Virtues are not just a chart on the wall that you check off every day. They require some self-knowledge, some depth psychology, to see if this is really who you are.

The doctrine of non-interference is an important part of the Brotherhoods' philosophy. The higher beings do not "help" people solve their problems, any more than teachers help their students with their homework lessons. And of course any kind of manipulation, mental or physical, is interference. We are here on this earth to learn certain lessons, and anyone who interferes with that process suffers the karmic consequences.

According to the Brotherhoods, there exist entities whose karma is so bad that they can no longer incarnate – they would just suffer some horrendous fate immediately. So they try to drag everybody else down with them. They interfere with human spiritual progress by telepathic suggestion. They are called "Black Mentalists." Their influences on our culture is shown by the color black – the black limousines, the most elegant formal dress in the highest diplomatic and social circles, and the black robes of the clergy.

We protect ourselves naturally from interference by these Black Mentalists by staying away from their emotional wavelengths – hate, greed, manipulation, and so forth. Also the Brotherhoods, while they won't <u>help</u> us with our problems, will <u>protect</u> us from interference. (No Black Mentalist has anywhere near the power of a human Master.) The Brotherhoods gave Richard a Protective Prayer. As Richard explained it, you don't pray vaguely for "help" or "guidance." There are plenty of spirit entities that would be only too glad to guide you – down the road to doom. You pray specifically to <u>Christ</u>, and only for <u>protection</u>. The Brotherhoods will respond, in the name of Christ (or Buddha, or Mohammed, or Moses).

The Protective Prayer helped me to deal with my spooky dreams. Sometimes I would encounter the presence of evil two or three levels deep, and it would take a tremendous exertion of will to struggle to the surface. Then I made the Protective Prayer a part of my being, so that I could use it in a dream. I found myself in one of those spooky dreams, two levels deep, and said "Dear Christ, please protect me." And I came bubbling up to the surface, instantly and effortlessly. The Protective Prayer has proved itself to me many times, both waking and dreaming.

The cosmology of the Brotherhoods as presented by Richard Kieninger is somewhat different from the Christian religion. Jesus and Christ are not the same being. Christ is the Archangel Melchizedek, the first-begotten Son of God. Jesus was a human Master, who let Christ use his body for His ministry. When John the Baptist baptized Jesus, that was when Christ took over his body. After the crucifixion, the body was repaired and given back to Jesus.

The Doomsday prophesied by the Brotherhoods of course didn't happen. But if you take everything they say as a working hypothesis, there is still plenty of value in their philosophy.

I haven't really begun to describe the Brotherhoods' philosophy, and I don't even want to try, because it is presented so well in *The Ultimate Frontier*. I would also recommend *Observations I-IV*, collections of essays by Richard Kieninger.

The Stelle Group no longer exists. The legacy of Richard Kieninger is preserved by The Adelphi Organization, P.O. Box 2423, Quinlan, Texas 75474. It contains a wealth of information to be tested.

I kept working on my psychological development until the fall of 1972, when I reached the psychological age of adulthood, or psychological age 18. At that point, I was totally satisfied with who I was. I had found happiness. I grew a beard to celebrate my manhood. I have never since been motivated to work actively on my psychological development, although I have experienced some psychological growth just through the experience of living.

Richard Kieninger said that it was possible to develop to psychological age 28, to develop clairvoyance and other attributes I wouldn't know about. But I am still the toad one hop from his hole. I think what I have accomplished is enough. Instead of getting into "spirituality," I think it is important to focus on psychological development. John Welwood, with "spiritual bypassing," supports me on this. Something that the people into "spirituality" don't know is that psychological maturity is a necessary first step in spiritual development.

CHAPTER 3

My Second Journey of Exploration

I had succeeded in my mission. Back in 1957, when people were running around screaming "Save the world!" I wanted to try to do something to help save the world, but I didn't see any immediate solution. I estimated that it would take 10 years to find a solution.

So here I was, in 1967, right on schedule. I had read books while I was in the Army. I had successfully gone through psychotherapy in New York. I had had a successful career as a computer programmer to pay for the psychotherapy. I had dropped out, walking the dunes in the solitude of Cape Cod winters, building a philosophy. I had spent a winter analyzing my own dreams, picking up where the psychiatrist had left off, and going beyond normal to reach a transition point where my "human nature" itself changed, from exclusive self-interest to compassion and altruism. I had truly discovered something that would save the world. I had discovered how to create a new kind of human being.

But when I tried to present my discoveries to the world, I was just met with opposition and contempt. This was all very traumatic for me. Years later, when a friend who was trying to help promote my work pushed my buttons, I exploded with anger. I still haven't resolved that trauma. I still don't really know what was going on.

First of all, in my career as a computer programmer, I was accustomed to being judged for what I actually did and accustomed to being recognized for my actual accomplishments. But the

85

reception for my philosophical discoveries was something totally different. I don't think anybody even mentioned anything I said.

The first of the irrational rejections was from the Hippies. They were at Haight-Ashbury at the same time that I was making my important discoveries during my dream winter of 1966-67, and immediately became the dominant force in our culture, because they could immediately put down, with a single word, anybody that opposed them.

So the moment I had a solution, my work of 10 years was instantly put down by the Hippies, who said, "If you haven't done drugs, what do you know?" They dismissed everything I was doing by calling it a "mind trip." They were "spiritual." They were superior. It was a kind of euphoria. Nothing factual was ever involved. It was all emotional.

I had worked for 10 years and had actually found an answer for our cultural problems. And then the Hippies came along, who had taken a drug that you could buy for 10 dollars, and instantly they were "superior." If I keep going on and on and on about the Hippies, it is because I am still traumatized by them.

Alan Watts wrote this wonderful put-down of Freud:

> I am not thinking of Freud's barbarous Id or Unconscious as the actual reality behind the facade of personality. Freud, as we shall see, was under the influence of a nineteenth-century fashion called "reductionism," a curious need to put down human culture and intelligence by calling it a fluky by-product of blind and irrational forces. They worked very hard, then, to prove that grapes can grow on thornbushes.
> (*The Book*, page 11)

This vicious put-down is from somebody who was supposed to be "spiritual."

I was so innocent. I did not know that I had a whole other journey of exploration ahead of me to learn what and how other persons in the culture were actually thinking, and why just having right answers was not good enough.

I present this second journey of exploration in chronological order, hoping that I can make some sense out of it.

Immediately after discovering the self-steering process, I just happened to run into a PhD psychologist I knew in the supermarket, and told her about my discovery.

Her response: "I don't think They would agree with you."

In 1967, I mentioned the name of Edgar Cayce to an elite scientist I knew, and he said, "Ha, ha, ha! That's so funny!" And 10 people at the table laughed with him.

In 1970, I sent the Table of Contents of "The Mental Scene" to an editor at Doubleday, who was a friend of a friend. She was very much interested in it.

The first reader at Doubleday called my manuscript "a primarily personal philosophy." Wasn't every philosophy a personal philosophy – Socrates, Aristotle, St. Augustine, Locke, Kant, Spinoza, Wittgenstein? I saw the word "personal" as a put-down. I had made discoveries – the nonauthoritarian approach to knowledge, the mental senses, the concept of psychological age, the change in "human nature" itself at the psychological age of puberty, and the self-steering process of dream analysis – discoveries of things that were not part of the cultural awareness and that applied to all human beings. I was also trying to bring into cultural awareness the discoveries of Carl Jung, especially "original experience," in which one is able to see the spiritual for oneself, and the discoveries of Edgar Cayce. These things certainly weren't "personal." I wouldn't have taken the trouble to write a book if I hadn't thought that everybody in the world should read it.

I didn't get to discuss that with her. She was in a position of power, where she got to say and I was only allowed to listen. I think she was probably an English major, fresh out of college. I don't think she had a clue to what I was saying.

I don't think the editor had a clue, either. I got to meet her when she came to Provincetown to visit our mutual friend. I was having an argument with my friend on my statement, "You can't make a move without a value system," and she had no comment to make, I assumed because she didn't understand what we were saying.

Later, I dreamed that she held me in an iron grip and dragged me down to Hell. Yes, of course, she had the power.

The reader said that the book should be more "intuitive." I wanted to dispute that. The part about dream analysis was very much intuitive. But again, she was in a position of power that couldn't be talked back to.

I think what she meant by "intuitive" was that I should write something that the Hippies would want to read. The Hippies so dominated the culture at the time that the only market seen for books trying to advance the culture had to be the Hippies.

What the publishers didn't know, and what I didn't have the presence of mind to tell them, was that there was a huge interest in my book from responsible people living in suburbia. These people really got excited about what I was doing, starting in the 1960s, when I was still working on the problem.

These were conventional people, but they, too, were aware of our cultural dilemmas and looking for solutions. And they were smart enough not to buy the stuff that the Hippies were trying to sell them.

I think that Doubleday would have been the perfect publisher to reach these people. But there was never any intelligent discussion on this subject. There was only the decree of the first reader that there was no market for this book.

It always bothered me that my work was called "personal." Couldn't they see that I was saying things that applied to the culture in general, such as how to change the human being? I see now that by moving outside the culture, I had moved into everybody's out-group, and that calling my works "personal" was only a polite way of saying that. Ideas that would be readily accepted coming from persons of the highest status have to be rejected and even ridiculed if they are coming from a member of the out-group.

But there was never any discussion of my ideas, never any rational evaluation of what I was saying. It was all this other stuff.

A couple of people told me, "You have a lot of nerve telling us you know the truth." This is such a complex set of assumptions combined with a threat that I would bore you analyzing it. There was no discussion of any factual thing that I said that they might have disagreed with, only this. I still don't know how to deal with it.

One of those people, a PhD psychologist, said, almost in the next sentence, "But you certainly know psychology." So right away she was contradicting herself.

She went on to tell me I was just "a guy." But weren't Aristotle and Freud and all those guys who made cultural advancements just "guys?" I had to go deep into my thought process just as I was writing this to try to explain this. Those people who are famous for making cultural innovations are not seen as ordinary people. They are seen as "great" people, an elevated kind of person, who is like a god. They are worshipped. They are like what our parents were to us when we were small children. They are like gods to us. We are in awe of them. We can't just hang out with them and have a conversation with them. We just have to listen to what they say and not speak unless spoken to. We are supposed to be like children in their presence.

I actually experienced this with a famous person, when I wanted to add my experience to what he was saying. I was given the social signal by an authoritarian person that my input was improper.

So, in the computer field, I was given recognition for having solutions to problems, but in the field of cultural innovation, I had to attain godhood first – or actually be viewed with contempt for presuming to have that status.

I was reminded of a traumatic experience I had had when I was 5. There was some problem by the side of the road in front of our house, probably a car stuck in the mud. I saw the solution, but when I tried to tell the grownups, they said, "Don't bother us! Can't you see we have a problem?" Eventually they saw the same solution, and it worked, and I was terribly hurt by it.

But in my 30s, I could see that the child was rejected because he had no status. I was reliving that psychological problem by presenting my solutions to the culture from a position of no status. What I needed to do was to go back to computer programming and gain a reputation as a "computer genius."

One phone call was all I needed to get a job at Wang Laboratories, which had bought out my former company. In the years 1974 to 1976, I wrote the key commercial software for the Wang 2200 – all Sort Utilities, KFAM versions 2-7 (Keyed File Access Method, file indexing software), and RPL (Report Program Language – I invented the language and wrote the compiler).

But my name was not on any of it. This was because when I had been assigned as the maintenance programmer on the original KFAM, which had bugs in it, my phone started ringing constantly. I couldn't get my work done with my phone ringing constantly. So all communications on my software were directed to the Technical Information Center, 3 guys who were able to handle most of them wonderfully and bring only a very few to my attention.

Of course this defeated my original purpose of being recognized as a "computer genius," but I was a year and a half into my employment at Wang, focusing on the job, and I had forgotten completely my original purpose.

I became a legend at Wang Laboratories after I left the company. But to the world at large I was still an unknown.

At some time during the Hippie era, I was having a conversation about my new civilization with a guy at Ciro's bar. He was very excited about it and kept asking me questions about it, for almost half an hour. And then he turned away to his beer and said, "Strange!"

I thought at the time that he was just a Hippie doing a number on me. But years later, I realized that I really was strange. I had become the fabulous weirdo that I had envisioned when I set out to develop my human potential.

In 1972, a friend of mine was looking for *The Ultimate Frontier* by Eklal Kueshana in her favorite bookstore on Charles Street in Boston. She said they had it UNDER THE COUNTER. It was too close to Mass. General and M.I.T. and other centers of physicalism.

In 1973, I read in *Harvard Magazine* that Freud was "out." A psychology professor was quoted as saying he wasn't familiar with Freud. That would have been disastrous to his academic status in the days when Freud was "in." It really communicated the message that Freud was "out."

In 1975, I wrote to the Menninger Clinic, offering them the 880 pages of my dream winter. They replied with a very polite letter, saying that they weren't interested.

In 1977, I took a beginning course in psychology. It wasn't about the psychology that I knew. It was mostly about brain chemistry and the nervous system.

I made enough money at Wang so that I could spend 7 years rewriting "The Mental Scene," to become *Re-Educating Myself*, with $5000 left over to print the book. By 1980, I had the first chapter written. Most people thought it was great. A few people didn't like it, including one editor who rejected it twice. My own self-criticism is that the chapter was a defensive mechanism, to write something that couldn't possibly be rejected. I didn't understand that I was not being rejected for what I said, but for my status in society.

In 1980, I met Otto Begus, Chairman of the Philosophy Department at Morgan State University. He was a summer tenant at our family property in Truro.

My father introduced us. He said, "Otto is a philosopher," and to Otto he said, "My son is writing a book on philosophy."

Otto asked, "What school of philosophy are you?"

"Now I am in trouble," was my answer. Then I recovered and said that I had once read that the way to study philosophy was to go out in the world with a notebook. That was my school. He supported me from that moment on.

But unlike the Professor of Astronomy who introduced John Couch Adams to the Astronomer Royal, Otto was out of touch with what his colleagues were doing in the field of philosophy. He was doing the real philosophy, the application of the mind to the living of life. He didn't seem to know, and I didn't know until I bought a philosophy textbook in 2021, that American academic philosophers limited themselves to "pure thought" – abstract thinking. They didn't even use evidence.

So Otto was always complaining about the poor quality of material in philosophy textbooks, and I was set up to be rejected by the in-group thinking of professional philosophers.

In 1981, I was invited to speak at my Harvard 25th Reunion on a panel on "Alternative Views of Success," one of my few moments of recognition.

In 1981, a person badly in need of psychological help gleefully informed me of *The Myth of Mental Illness*, by Thomas Szasz (pronounced "saws"). I could see, by the word "myth" in the title, that this was not going to be an accurate scholarly piece of work, and when he linked psychiatry to alchemy twice and astrology 4 times in the first 2 pages, that confirmed it. Any freshman class in critical thinking should be able to expose the invalid arguments in this book. But for people threatened by the idea of psychotherapy, this has become a best-seller.

In 1982, I submitted the first 8 chapters of *Re-Educating Myself* to literary agent Scott Meredith for a critical review, for a price of $200. And for my $200, I got $5000 worth of psychological damage.

The graduate students that reviewed my book used half a dozen words that I had to look up in the dictionary, and they all meant "stupid." In order to do that, they ignored every intelligent thing I had to say. It seemed that they had a psychological need to declare their intellectual superiority. They could bully me because they were in a position of power where I had no right of rebuttal. This was a psychological blow to me at the time, I guess because I was desperately looking for recognition. I was hoping that somebody would "discover" me. I had paid for an honest appraisal, and instead they "did a number on me," as the Hippies used to say. I complained to Scott Meredith, but he didn't care.

Later that year, this put-down was totally reversed by one of the most important people in the publishing industry, Donald Klopfer, the founder of Random House, a man whose name was on 3 of the 6 most influential books of my life (Modern Library Series). An old girlfriend of mine, whose godmother happened to be married to him, took my manuscript to him. She was somewhat of a con artist, and approached him with the pitch, "This may be too radical for you," whereupon he replied that he had created the name "Random House" to mean "We will publish anything, if we think it is good."

He thought it was good. He told her, "With the right kind of hype, this could sell a million copies." And he sent the manuscript off to Random House.

But he had already sold his company to RCA, and they rejected the manuscript in spite of his recommendation. This was upsetting to him. It also might have been damaging to his reputation. So he refused me permission to quote him. I have honored his request during his lifetime, but the quote is the truth, it is the most important thing that was ever said about me in my lifetime, it is etched into my brain, and I am still trying to prove that he was right.

Actually, in all fairness to Donald Klopfer, as corporate America took over the publishing houses, the whole philosophy of publishing changed, from publishing the best books to guaranteeing the maximum profits, with predefined markets, credentials, and platforms determining a book's publishability.

Unlike Donald Klopfer, I was greatly relieved that RCA didn't want to publish my book. A friend, an uncle, and I had all had bad experiences with RCA. I really didn't want to put my life's work in their hands.

I think that RCA, along with Doubleday, was trying to tell me, "Write something the Hippies will want to read." Really I was writing something that responsible people wanted to read, to advance our culture. The Chief of Security at Wang Laboratories wanted to read my book.

In 1983, I spent 8 hours in the Provincetown Public Library reading about "Evolution" and related subjects in the *Encyclopedia Britannica*. I discovered that there were species that had appeared more quickly in geological time than could be explained by the slow process of adaptation. This shook my faith in Darwin's Theory of Evolution.

When I expressed doubts about the Theory of Evolution, people twisted that to mean that I questioned the fact of evolution itself and compared me to the Holocaust Revisionists.

So I used "evolution-1" to mean the fact of evolution and "evolution-2" to mean the Theory of Evolution, when I wrote *The Mental Environment*.

In *Dirty Science*, I called the theory "Darwin's theory of unintelligent design" and used the word "evolution" only to mean the fact of evolution.

In 1985, after 22 rejections, I decided to self-publish *Re-Educating Myself*. I had already bought an IBM proportional-spacing electric typewriter with that thought in mind. My nephew-in-law, David Cox, did the cover picture. My partner of many years, Ailene Wright, designed the cover and typeset anything I couldn't type with my typewriter. With the help of a dozen books on self-publishing, especially *The Self-Publishing Manual* by Dan Poynter, I managed to publish the book myself.

I learned about the extreme snobbery in the publishing industry against self-publishers. A self-published author was not an "author" and not eligible to join The Authors Guild. A first-edition paperback was not a "book." The major reviewers snubbed self-published books, so I went to small presses for reviews, and got good reviews from several of them.

In 1985, a neighbor in Provincetown told me that he had placed a copy of *Re-Educating Myself* on the desk of the editor of *The New York Times Book Review*.

In 1985, a friend showed *Re-Educating Myself* to her father, who was head of the philosophy department at a prestigious college. He rejected it abruptly and abusively, without even looking at it. "He had to dominate," she told me.

In 1985, I began making the rounds of the bookstores on Cape Cod. The manager of the Booksmith in Hyannis told me, "Books like this don't sell." And I replied, "There has never been a book like this, and we don't know if it will sell." They sold about 10 copies, before they went out of business.

Walking into a bookstore to sell my own book I always felt was like walking to the guillotine. Norman Mailer never had to walk into a bookstore to sell his own books. They could see me coming.

Nevertheless, the Provincetown Bookshop was a steady customer, the book sold in Chatham because of Donald Klopfer, people always seemed to find it among the thousands of books in Parnassus, and I even made it occasionally into Trident Booksellers in Boston. I was selling books, but only a few at a time and in a limited area.

I did have 3 distributors, but they didn't sell very many copies in all the rest of the country. The book sold a little over 700 copies, disastrous by publishing industry standards, but not bad, I have been told, for a self-published book.

In 1986, I offered *Re-Educating Myself* to philosophy departments for $7.95, 20% discount. I received orders mostly from colleges I had never heard of, and some with personal checks. The highest-ranking college that responded was ranked about #85. One would have thought that Harvard, with its $30 billion endowment, could have afforded to spend $7.95 to find out what this new philosophy was all about, but no.

"It all has to do with status," I complained to my friends.

"Of course it all has to do with status," they replied. "Didn't you know that?"

No, I didn't.

In 1988, I sent a copy of *Re-Educating Myself*, along with an angry letter, to Michael Murphy of Esalen Institute, the founder of "The Human Potential Movement." I argued that the "The" was false in giving the impression that his was the only movement working on the human potential, when I had begun 8 years before he began and had actually achieved something in that area, namely discovering how "human nature" itself could be changed. He responded to my angry letter with high praise for my book, saying, "The philosophy in your book is wonderful. Congratulations!" And he gave me permission to quote him. He even said that he was going to share my book with friends, but I suspect they were all Hippies, because I never heard anything from any of them.

(After I wrote the letter to Michael Murphy) I read somewhere that Aristotle had said that the way to happiness was to develop one's potential as a human being. But in the very next paragraph he claimed to know exactly what the human potential was. At least I know more than Aristotle, by saying that I don't know what the human potential is.

In 1991, I had learned that academic people expected to be offered a free "examination copy" of a book, so I sent an ad to 2000 philosophy departments offering them a free book, with the headline, "AN ACTIVITY WITH NO NAME?" and quoting a passage from the book:

> What are the needs of man? What is man? What is life? What is the purpose of man's life, if any? Who am I? … How do I know what to believe? Can I use logic? Can I trust my own mind?
>
> I recognized these questions and the search for fundamental truths as something that used to be called "philosophy," before the word was appropriated by an academic subculture to describe some highly specialized intellectual exercise. …
>
> In an age of specialization the thing needed most to solve the most important problems was some general philosophy, which by definition of words had ceased to exist, leaving a blind spot in the cultural thinking. I was engaged in an activity that had no name.
>
> (*Re-Educating Myself*, First Edition, pages 18-19)

They all knew what I was talking about. My little post office box was absolutely stuffed with responses for 3 days straight. I sent out about 100 copies of the book. I actually climbed up the social ladder, to reach the university ranked #35. And then I never received any feedback from any of them. I thought of it as a "deafening silence."

In 1991, Ann Sayre Wiseman "discovered" me for the Association for the Study of Dreams (ASD). I presented my paper on "The Self-Steering Process" at their annual conference that summer.

I thanked Robert van de Castle for accepting my paper. His reply: "We are always looking for new material."

Apparently, nobody at the conference knew that Carl Jung had described the self-steering process in a paper published in 1931, although many of the dreamworkers there knew about it and seemed to have discovered it independently, as I had.

Rita Dwyer thanked me for my presentation.

There were 2 distinct political groups at the conference. One that I shall call the "intuitive" group observed dreams themselves with the mental senses. The other, which I shall call the "academic" group, limited their observations to the evidence of the physical senses, and so studied only the words people used in reporting their dreams.

A man in a Hawaiian shirt sat down with me one day at lunch. He asked me, "Have you ever considered that dreams might come from God?"

It turned out that he was a Catholic priest. If he had been in uniform, I would have dismissed the question as part of his religious doctrine. But because he was just an innocent man in a Hawaiian shirt, I gave the question some thought.

Dreams came from the unconscious. But the fact that it was unconscious meant that we didn't know where dreams came from. Yes, to my knowledge, dreams could very well come from God.

Are we studying the TV set to find out where the programs are coming from?

In 1995, I was told by a guy on the Internet that Freud was "brilliantly refuted" in 1961. He didn't name any book, so I assumed he was referring to *The Myth of Mental Illness*, by Thomas Szasz.

In 1995, I was in a discussion group on the Internet with an expert manipulator. He was quick to point out, as all liars are, that I couldn't call him a "liar" without being able to prove that his false statements were intentional.

And I was quick to point out, with my mathematics, that if he was just innocently making false statements, then half of them would be favorable. But the fact that all of his false statements were unfavorable showed intention on his part. The odds of making 7 false statements, all defamatory, just by chance, would be 1 in 128, or $p = .0078+$. Scientifically this is significant, to say that this didn't happen by chance. There had to be some other force working. This had to be done with malice.

Also on the Internet around 1995, I told a PhD psychologist about the psychological age of puberty, and she replied, "Maslow must have said that." I was duped by her into researching Maslow. I should have required of her, if she wanted to maintain the credibility of her PhD status, that she give me a book and page number and an exact quote.

As it was, my idea of research is spending a couple of hours on the Internet looking things up. I reasoned that Maslow couldn't have observed people going through the psychological age of puberty because he wasn't observing the psychological growth process taking place. He was only observing individuals at a fixed point in their lives, namely their total achievement. Some of these individuals may have achieved psychological maturity, but he didn't observe them going through the process and gave no indication that such a transition point existed.

Maslow envisioned world leaders sitting around a peace table and envisioned that the way to achieve this higher mental state was through peak experiences and cosmic consciousness. This of course resonated with the Hippies, who immediately made him famous.

But no, the way to having world leaders sitting around a peace table is through people achieving the compassion and altruism that comes with reaching the psychological age of puberty.

In the years 1999 to 2007, I wrote and self-published *The Mental Environment: (Mostly about Mind Pollution)*, describing the network of lies from which I had to extricate myself in my quest for a new civilization. We are immersed in a sea of other people's thoughts. The culture is still not aware of that. If fish had a language, they would have no word for "water." When I went to bookstores, I would wave my hand around at all the books, to explain what I meant by "the mental environment."

By "mind pollution," I meant inaccuracies in those thoughts. I was borrowing a term used by Pete Seeger. Now the culture is waking up to mind pollution, with the words "misinformation" and "disinformation."

Living in Hanover, New Hampshire, I had access to the Dartmouth College Libraries. It was the first time in my life that I did any serious research. I was able to order from the archives the original works of John B. Watson, in my efforts to see why psychologists had abandoned the study of the mind. I was able to read the original work of Niles Eldredge, describing how some species had evolved more quickly in geological time than could be explained by the slow process of adaptation.

I found *There Is a River: The Story of Edgar Cayce* by Thomas Sugrue in the Dartmouth library. I also found *The Ultimate Fontier* by Eklal Kueshana in their catalog, but the book itself was mysteriously missing, as I had previously discovered with publications about or by Richard Kieninger and The Stelle Group. There are people who don't want us to read this stuff.

The Dartmouth library also had every issue of the *Journal of Parapsychology*, but as I learned, when I read a smear of parapsychology in their beginning psychology textbook, their freshman students were given the social message that they weren't supposed to read it.

From the Hanover Public Library I found *Consilience*, by Edward O. Wilson, saying that if we all thought like biologists, we would have "consilience," and smearing other modes of thought to achieve that end.

I was able to see some wonderful examples of dirty politics from my Representative in Congress, Charlie Bass.

I was able to take a course in Social Psychology at Dartmouth, wherein I learned of Machiavellian tactics used to manipulate people. I was made aware of the book, *Studies in Machiavellianism*, by Richard Christie and Florence L. Geis, documenting scientific studies of people's ability to manipulate each other.

I lived on a dirt road, where I couldn't see my nearest neighbor. I could only hear them when they fired their guns. It was so quiet most of the time that I could hear the wings of a crow whooshing through the air over my head. If I heard a noise in the summer it was thunder and in the winter it was the snowplow. I experienced the same kind of withdrawal that I had experienced in the solitude of Cape Cod winters.

In my 45th reunion report to Harvard in 2001, I said that I didn't give money to Harvard because Harvard supported "scientism," as I called it at the time, the belief that there was no reality beyond the physical. Then I decided to give the money that I was not giving to Harvard to some worthy cause. I looked up "J.B. Rhine" on the Internet, and found "The Rhine Research Center." I sent them my check for $1000, along with a copy of my reunion report and an explanatory letter.

As soon as the mail was able to reach them, I received an enthusiastic phone call from Sally Rhine Feather, the daughter of J.B. Rhine and Executive Director of The Rhine Research Center. Of course she shared my views that the psychic and the spiritual were real and that these things had been ignorantly dismissed by the academic establishment. I wanted to work at The Rhine as a volunteer, but first I had to finish *The Mental Environment*. So we entered into an email correspondence.

I told Sally (as I called her, not "Dr. Feather") about the name "GERALD FORD CARTER" that I had printed on a piece of paper, long before the historical importance of either of these men was recognized. I asked her if there were dating methods that would determine when this was printed. Her answer was shocking and deserves repetition here:

> No, we do not seek to verify or get proof of the veracity or the paranormal quality of any of our reports, as was once the custom back in the old psychical research days. The early psychical researchers went to enormous effort to obtain highly documented cases, and books are filled with excellent cases that could stand for as much scientific proof as case material could ever be. And you know what? No one in the scientific world seemed to pay much attention. (Not that they pay so much attention to scientific research results either, I hasten to add).
> (from an email of September 20, 2001)
> (*The Mental Environment*, page 245)

And I continue with my own commentary in *The Mental Environment*:

> If scientific people aren't paying much attention to research results, then what are they paying attention to? What is their source of information that supercedes research results? And if some other source of information is more important, are they doing science?
> If scientific people ignore something, they disqualify themselves from holding a scientific opinion on it. Ignoring things also leads to ignorance, which is the opposite of what academia is all about. And yet with their enormous status, they are able to get away with it.
> (*The Mental Environment*, page 245)

In 2004, I learned that Carl Jung had mentioned the self-steering process in a paper published in 1931. But he didn't stress the importance of it. I am stressing the importance of it. It is my opinion that he didn't stress its importance because he was writing in an era when only professionals were supposed to interpret people's dreams.

In 2006, I presented a paper on "The Mental Senses" at the annual conference of the International Association for the Study of Dreams (IASD). Sally Rhine Feather, Robert van de Castle, and one other celebrity were giving a presentation in the next room, so all I got, it seemed, was the overflow crowd. But Rita Dwyer again thanked me for my presentation. That was important to me.

At least I had a chance to meet Sally Rhine Feather and say "Hello."

In 2007, at some time before I published *The Mental Environment*, I was made aware of Frederick Crews, whose arguments against psychotherapy were so brilliant that I didn't dare argue with him. But he confessed that he had never been through psychotherapy himself.

Would you respect a book on climbing Mt. Everest from somebody who had never climbed it, or on mathematics from a person who had never studied it, or on sailboat racing from a person who didn't know how to sail? It seems that these people that have never experienced psychotherapy, or have failed at it, feel that they have an equal right to express their opinion, along with people who are knowledgeable in the field. And of course they have an equal right to express their opinion. The problem is that people who really want to believe, who are threatened by psychotherapy, believe them. So they are doing a disservice to society. The more books they sell, the greater the disservice they are doing.

In 2007, I moved from Hanover, New Hampshire, back to Provincetown, thinking I had a better chance to market *The Mental Environment* in Provincetown. But Provincetown had changed, from creative people living at the poverty level to a community of rich homosexuals. The rent I had to pay was enormous. I did manage to find a few old friends for my book party, but that was it.

I tried to get a publicist for *The Mental Environment*, without much luck. The publicist I did get, for a lot of money, didn't really seem to have a clue to what the book was all about, and made inappropriate connections for me.

I submitted the book for the Benjamin Franklin Awards and was told it was "unacceptable" because it was printed ragged-right. Actually ragged-right is easier to read than right-justified, because the spacing of the letters is exactly the same throughout. But the people in the publishing industry didn't seem to know that. I was learning that the publishing industry had its own in-group opinions, attitudes, and beliefs (OABs), to which all writers of books were expected to conform.

One academic person bought 30 copies of *The Mental Environment*, I assume for a class. Other than that, sales were poor. I don't think I sold many more than 100 copies. But over the years, I have noticed that it has continued to sell a few copies from the "New & Used" on Amazon.

In 2009, I moved to Durham, North Carolina, to work as a volunteer at The Rhine Research Center. This is where I learned really how serious the academic prejudice was against the psychic and the spiritual.

A visiting lecturer on communication with the dead complained that he was shunned by his colleagues, who pointed to their heads to indicate that he was crazy.

A graduate student was advised not to write a paper on parapsychology, because it could be career-ending.

A man came to The Rhine one day with his son, whose science project had been given a failing grade because it was on psychic and spiritual phenomena.

Academic people who expressed a serious interest in the psychic or the spiritual were treated by their colleagues as if they were mentally incompetent, and denied publication, funding, and employment. Tenured professors who could not be fired were shunned. It was equivalent to what excommunication was in the Dark Ages.

Wikipedia was definitely biased towards the physical. It called parapsychology a "pseudoscience." A former President of the Parapsychological Association, Nancy Zingrone, had tried to correct them on this without any success. If she had failed, as a person of the very highest status, I saw that I was not likely to succeed. So I dug deeper, to see if there was any rational basis for Wikipedia's opinion of parapsychology.

What I discovered was a report issued in 1988 by the National Academy of Sciences that concluded:

> The committee finds no scientific justification from research conducted over a period of 130 years for the existence of parapsychological phenomena.
> (*Enhancing Human Performance: Issues, Theories, and Techniques*, edited by Daniel Druckman and John A. Swets, 1988, page 22)

Actually, the committee DID NOT LOOK AT the research of 130 years. The report contained only 5 references to the peer-reviewed *Journal of Parapsychology*, which dates back to 1937, and no references either to the peer-reviewed British journal, which dates back to 1882, or to the peer-reviewed European journal. It does not even mention the name "J.B. Rhine," let alone refute his findings and the people who replicated them throughout the world. The scope of the study clearly did not support its sweeping conclusion.

There is literally a ton of evidence of parapsychological phenomena at The Rhine Research Center.

One of the in-group norms that I carried over from my Harvard experience was never to be impressed by anybody. But I was truly impressed by the credentials of the leaders of the National Academy of Sciences. How such an impressive group of people could have been duped into publishing this obviously false report was a mystery to me.

So I wrote a letter to Ralph J. Cicerone, the President of the National Academy of Sciences at the time, with help from Sally Rhine Feather, who advised me not to use the words "farce" or "sham," and John Palmer, Editor of the *Journal of Parapsychology*, saying that this blatantly invalid report was potentially damaging to the reputation of the National Academy of Sciences, that this didn't happen on his watch, and that it would be to his great credit if he would look into the matter with a view to correcting the serious omissions and unsupported conclusion of the report.

In his reply to me, he offered to find a "knowledgeable disinterested" person to investigate the subject. I couldn't help thinking that that might be as difficult as finding a disinterested person on the subject of psychedelic drugs or the Presidential election of 2000.

Nothing ever came of this. The National Academy of Sciences will be forever recorded in the annals of folly for publishing this report, along with the people who asserted that nothing heavier than air could fly, or the person who said in the 1880s that the Patent Office should be closed because nothing more could possibly be invented, with the important difference that this particular folly is totally documented.

In 2011, I was having an interesting discussion of philosophy with a philosophy professor who came to visit The Rhine. But then he broke off the conversation abruptly and said, "But we have to do that other stuff."

In 2013, I sent letters to the presidents or chancellors of the 137 top-ranked colleges and universities in the United States, complaining that the academic establishment supported what has been called "physicalism," "scientism," "materialism," or "reductionism," the belief that there is no reality beyond the physical. I described the invalid arguments supporting that belief, especially the threat that serious interest in the psychic or spiritual could be career-ending for an academic person.

I approached them as persons of the highest status in their in-group, who had the greatest ability to make changes. I don't know whether they liked the expression "in-group" applied to the academic community, but I hoped that at least they would give it some thought.

I received acknowledgements that 39 of them had read my letter. Most of them seemed to be under the impression that there was still academic freedom. Four of them said that all subjects were debatable at their institutions. The catch there is that the psychic and the spiritual are not part of their curricula, and therefore not subjects to be debated.

One president agreed with me, but the publications she referred to were totally incomprehensible to me. I realized that academic people were functioning in an environment of books. Books were their reality. Because I hadn't read all the books they had read, I was lost.

My letter was published as a Guest Editorial with the title "Physicalism" in the *Journal of Parapsychology*, Fall 2013, Volume 77, Number 2. This led to a speaking engagement, on a panel on the same general subject, at the Annual Convention of the Parapsychological Association in 2014.

In 2019, through BookBaby, I published *Dirty Science: How Unscientific Methods Are Blocking Our Cultural Advancement.* Seeing that everybody who has ever been to college in the United States needs to read this book, it hasn't sold very many copies.

I sent copies of *Dirty Science*, with copies of good reviews, to the presidents or chancellors of the same top-ranked 137 colleges and universities in the United States, and received encouraging letters from a few of them, including the President of Harvard, the President of the University of California system, and the President's Room at Princeton.

Dirty Science won 4 awards and had some good reviews. But there were also reviewers who were biased towards physicalism, who had to change the facts so that they could smear me. I got rid of most of them with the word "misrepresentation."

I advertised *Dirty Science* on Facebook, but the smear tactics of the trolls were much more powerful than my advertising. Sometimes I answered them with words like "invalid," but I don't know whether that helped.

In 2019, my partner Alice retyped *Re-Educating Myself* in digital format as a birthday present for me. Because it contained language which had been called "sexist," I spent some time changing the language and adding a preface, and published this Second Edition through BookBaby in 2021. It sold a few copies and reached a few people in countries where it had never reached before.

In 2021, I bought a philosophy textbook, published in 2011. It defined "philosophy" as only pure thought, of an abstract nature. "Philosophy" did not even include evidence, it said.

In 2022, the audiobook of *Dirty Science*, narrated by Sarasvati Ishaya, was published on Amazon.

In 2023, I saw in the news that the Bulletin of the Atomic Scientists had set their Doomsday Clock to 90 seconds before midnight, because of the war in Ukraine. This is an organization, formed in 1947, that has been dedicated to the survival of the species, the same as I have been, against "man-made existential threats, including nuclear risk, climate change, and disruptive technologies." The principals in their organization are persons of the very highest status, including 4-term California Governor Edmund G. Brown, Jr. and two heads of state. They were just the kind of important people I needed, in order to gain recognition for my work.

So I sent them several emails telling them how I had found a solution through psychotherapy and how I had discovered how "human nature" itself could be changed. And I received no response from them. I did receive a phone message saying, "Thank you for the letters," but because I am hard of hearing, I didn't know whether it was from them.

I saw that one of their principals, Lynn Eden, had made the statement, "The answer lies not in individual psychology..." But there was no explanation to back that up, and no indication that she had any qualifications to say anything about individual psychology. I even bought her book, but again there was no indication in it that she knew anything about individual psychology.

I complained about this dismissal of individual psychology in another email, but received no response.

This does not include every book I read or every discovery I made, in re-educating myself in the ways of the world, but I think I have covered all the main events.

So, what have I learned in this second journey of exploration?

By moving outside the culture, I was in everybody's out-group. I learned how powerful the social laws were.

My one voice was drowned out by the Hippies, who dominated the culture with their "spirituality" for many years.

Some people were threatened by what I was saying, and their psychological defenses blocked me, as in "You have a lot of nerve telling us you know the truth."

Some people in positions of power took advantage of the fact that I had no opportunity for rebuttal, in order to smear me, to satisfy their own psychological needs.

The publishing industry had gone from publishing works of merit to publishing works that would guarantee them profits, with predefined markets, platforms, and credentials. They had every right to do this, because they had been going bankrupt the other way.

They won't even look at a manuscript unless it is submitted by a literary agent. This places the burden of screening the large volume of unsolicited manuscripts upon the literary agents, who receive only a tiny percentage of the gross income. This is unfair to the literary agents, who are forced to reject good manuscripts in the blink of an eye, and unfair to the many authors of these good manuscripts, who are forced to publish their books themselves and endure the status-snobbery of the publishing industry.

I think what we need are charitable organizations, foundations for the arts, culture, and education (ACE), that will take the time to go through the 1.7 million books that are independently published every year, pick out the ones they think have merit, and bring them to the attention of the culture.

The main problem with *Re-Educating Myself* was that most people did not understand what I was saying. It was beyond their ken. It wasn't what they learned in school. They didn't know what to make of it. They had to change it into something they could understand – and reject. I complained that most people couldn't read the same words I wrote (even though it was written at an 11th-grade reading level). It is really hard to convince people of the merits of a book, when they don't understand what you are saying.

My partner Alice does not read this kind of stuff. She would much rather be reading high-quality fiction or British mysteries. She has never been through psychotherapy, and she doesn't believe in the spiritual. But she has taken the time to read, and has made an effort to understand, all of my books. She had the best reading comprehension of *Re-Educating Myself* of anybody. I would have given most people less than 40% for reading comprehension. I am just saying that if everybody had made the same effort that Alice did, they would have understood it better.

But there is a certain status-snobbery among persons of status. They view books by persons of no recognizable status as "these kinds of books" and not worthy of their attention. One university administrator was amazed that he could find no typos, spelling errors, or grammatical errors in the book. Apparently he put it in the category of "these kinds of books" to start with, and then that was all he was looking for. He didn't seem to notice that I had actually said anything, because of course it was beneath him to learn anything from "these kinds of books."

The same authoritarianism that I was opposing was operating against me in the culture. Only persons of status were allowed to present them with "the truth." Persons of no status trying to present "the truth" were considered arrogant, uppity, and not knowing their place.

They didn't understand that persons of status in industry had hired me to solve their problems and give them the right answers. I was always at what I called "Level 0" there, meaning I had nobody beneath me, but persons of the highest status always treated me with the highest respect, always recognized my solutions on their merits, and of course always made huge profits from my labors.

But even if I had overcome all these obstacles, the main problem was that the academic community had failed to live up to its claims. I had been led to believe, when I was at Harvard, that academic people were unbiased and open-minded, unlike religious people, who had prejudices and whose minds were closed to anything outside of their religious doctrine. I had thought that I could present my solutions for humanity to the academic community and that those solutions would be evaluated impartially on their own merit. This is not at all the reality of academia.

First of all, there are large gaps in philosophy, psychology, and sociology, where there is nobody expert in what I am doing. There is nobody I can go to with my discoveries.

And then there are the prejudices against Sigmund Freud, Carl Jung, psychotherapy for themselves, dream analysis, the spiritual, spirit entities, psychic abilities, reincarnation, levitation, Edgar Cayce, and Richard Kieninger. I say "prejudices," because they are not supported by valid arguments, but by arguments that all academic people know are illegitimate. Academic people are not living up to their own academic standards, they are not aware of that, and they are not leading our culture into knowledge, but away from knowledge. In the next chapter, I will track the historical record of how this happened.

There is one thing I haven't mentioned, because it didn't happen. Nobody except for me ever found anything wrong with *Re-Educating Myself*. Yes, they misrepresented me, and they didn't read the same words that I wrote, in order to reject me, but they never accurately refuted anything I said in this book.

CHAPTER 4

The Closing of the American Mind

I am using here the title of a book that was the top bestseller in 1987, because it describes exactly what happened to my solution for the survival of the species. The 1987 book argued that the downfall of our culture was because we didn't study the classics any more, as we used to. Actually, my Latin teacher said that better in 1950. The critics were mystified as to why the book was a #1 bestseller. I think it was because of the title. It resonates with people. They know that our culture is going downhill, and they are eager to know why, and here is an answer — but not in that book.

I have a chronology of specific events to show how the American mind is closing, the culture is going downhill, and we are actually moving AWAY from survival of the species, at least by my solution.

I define the "culture," for the purposes of this discussion, as our American accredited academic establishment. They officially determine what is "knowledge" in our culture. By the rules of our authoritarian upbringing, they are the teachers, and therefore they are right, and anybody that disagrees with them is wrong. They function as an in-group, and some of their opinions, attitudes, and beliefs are strictly enforced. It can be career-ending to disagree with this group-conformity. I see "the American mind" as the minds of these academic people, and where they are rigidly bound to this group-conformity.

Our accredited academic institutions turn out about two million college graduates per year, all of whom are influenced, and many indoctrinated, by the in-group opinions, attitudes, and beliefs of their academic teachers. These college graduates then become the upper classes of our culture and the people responsible for our mainstream information and knowledge. Yes, there are the Hippies, and yes, there are outsiders like myself, but the people with the official knowledge of our culture, the people who are called in as "expert" witnesses, are the people with the academic credentials.

We have the expression *"alma mater"* for one's college. It means "dear mother" in Latin. You do not criticize a person's mother. I am wondering whether the 80 million college graduates in the United States see their *alma mater* as sacred, and beyond criticism?

I had been led to believe, as I said, that academic people were unbiased and open-minded, unlike religious people who had prejudices and rigid beliefs. I thought that academic people would read my book and evaluate it impartially. I thought they would welcome new knowledge. I was so innocent. I had no idea that the academic establishment was closed not only to my new knowledge, but to whole areas of knowledge that I had ventured into – Sigmund Freud, Carl Jung, psychotherapy as education, dream analysis, psychic abilities, the spiritual, Edgar Cayce, reincarnation, karma, levitation, Richard Kieninger, and Black Mentalists. And all of these taboos were supported by invalid arguments. And no academic person dared question these invalid arguments, because to do so would be career-ending.

I didn't know any of that when I published *Re-Educating Myself*, until I made my whole new journey of exploration. I didn't know I was going to have to do that, either. I want to present here the chronology of how the American mind became closed. Again, this does not replace what I said in *The Mental Environment* or *Dirty Science*. In some cases this is only a summary, and the full argument is in those other books. If you want to refute me, you will have to read everything I wrote.

So here I am, an individual with no visible (above the radar) status, standing against the massed credentialed minds of the American accredited academic establishment. What chance do I have? They are the teachers. They are the experts. Their view is accepted as the truth. Any view that is different is automatically assumed to be wrong.

So if you are looking at what I am doing as my status against theirs, you will see me as incredibly arrogant. No academic person has told me I am arrogant, but I have seen their looks of scorn and felt their silence.

I am reminded of a story told by the man who came to cut the hayfield at a place where I was staying in Maine. He had worked as a maintenance man at Cornell, and physicists were conducting some kind of experiment in the basement of a building, where they had to make a mark on the wall. And they couldn't understand why the marks were in such radically different places from one day to the next. While they were arguing about it one day, this maintenance man explained to them that they were making their marks on a sliding door, which was opened every night to take out the trash and then of course was closed in a slightly different position.

Well, he said, they looked at him like a wolf pack that was about to devour him. The maintenance man does not tell credentialed physicists where their experiment went wrong. We have a caste system in America. Those with bachelor's degrees have one level of status in our culture. Those with PhD degrees have a higher level. Those with PhD degrees are socially conditioned not to learn anything from people two levels below them. It is simply status-snobbery. Obviously this maintenance man had knowledge that they didn't have.

I am like the maintenance man. I am a person of no apparent status opposing the massed credentialed professionals of our accredited academic institutions. I would expect status-snobbery. I would never be so foolish as to argue against them in their areas of expertise. But this is even more difficult: I am trying to point out errors in entrenched thinking that has been forced upon them by threat of excommunication.

DISMISSING MESMERISM

Some people have the power to implant their thoughts into other people's minds. This is called "hypnotism," or "mesmerism," after Franz Anton Mesmer, who discovered the phenomenon in the late 1700s. I have read that Mesmer made a circus of it, and therefore he and his discovery were dismissed by the scientific establishment of his day. I have also read that King Louis XVI of France commissioned a study of it, which found Mesmer lacking in evidence. Hypnotism or mesmerism has been recognized at times by the academic establishment, but I think now it is generally ignored and on the list of things that are generally ridiculed in academia.

Mesmerism is a very real force. I have seen a friend, who played tackle on our football team, under hypnosis. He could not move a small folding chair when he was told that it weighed 2000 pounds. I have had my mind paralyzed by a yoga instructor when I got too friendly with his girlfriend, and I never spoke to her again.

These are extreme cases of mesmerism. What I am concerned with are its everyday uses, specifically in the academic community. I have observed that people with strong mentalities are able to confuse my thoughts or block my thought process. I call this "mind-scrambling" and "mind-jamming." I believe that some, many, or all people who are able to dominate have these powers. I believe that people who are able to dominate dominate in the academic community, and that this detracts from accurate knowledge.

This is "woo-woo" stuff. But why should "woo-woo" have any power as an argument, when every academic person knows that it is not a legitimate argument? There has to be some mental power conveyed with it.

All I am saying is that the academic community made a mistake when they rejected mesmerism. The subject needs to be studied in the academic community, especially as it affects the academic community and the accuracy of our cultural knowledge.

DUMPING THE SPIRITUAL

"Physicalism," the belief that there is no reality beyond the physical or what can be explained by known physical laws, originated roughly around 1870, when T.H. Huxley and others extended Darwin's Theory of Evolution to include the evolution of life itself from the primeval muck. With this extended Theory of Evolution, there was no need for a Creator to explain how living things came to exist on this planet. So God and the whole idea of a spiritual reality were just dumped.

It is important to differentiate between the fact of evolution and the Theory of Evolution, as I have said. Life on earth evolved over a period of more than a billion years, as has been scientifically determined. God did not create the earth and all living creatures in 6 days in 4004 BC, as is written in the Bible. It is only the mechanism of evolution that I am questioning: Did it happen by "random" mutation, or was there some intelligence behind it?

I have already pointed out that animal breeders know that it is impossible to go beyond the boundaries of a species to create another species, because the individuals near the norm for the species tend to be more robust than those near the outer limits of the species, which are more likely to be sterile. Ernst Mayr even had a fancy name for it, "genetic homeostasis."

Random mutation would favor those individuals at or near the norm, because they are more likely to have offspring and keep the species at or near the norm. Even with the stimulus of "punctuated equilibria," or sudden changes in the environment, this natural law would not change. A species could adapt, but not change into another species. As the biologist pointed out to me, the most likely effect of a major change in the environment would be extinction.

So if human intelligence is unable to create a new species, this is not likely to happen by random mutation. I think human intelligence has already created something that grows and reproduces naturally, but only with a great deal of intelligence, knowledge, and effort.

So, then, what intelligence with a knowledge of genetic engineering created all those species that already exist in nature? There is still a need to postulate a creator, not as the Bible said it happened, but in geological time, as the environment became ready to support each species.

In *Re-Educating Myself*, I did a little mathematical exercise to show the probability of putting a thousand things together randomly, to create the one combination that would become a living creature. Of course I had to make many wild approximations, but I made them all in favor of a living creature being created. I found that the probability of such a random creation taking place in the age of the universe would be more than a trillion trillion trillion trillion trillion trillion trillion trillion trillion trillion trillion trillion trillion trillion times less likely than the probability of dealing the perfect bridge hand in the perfect order on the first deal.

But living creatures are much more complicated than that. There are millions or billions or trillions of things that have to be put together in the right order to create a living creature. I couldn't find any figures for the simplest living creature, but for the single-celled creatures that I did find, the numbers started in the millions. So my little exercise of putting a thousand things together at random was way too low. The probability of putting a million things together randomly, where the probability of getting each step right is $1/2$, is $2^{-1000000}$. This is approximately $10^{-300000}$. This is so much less likely than putting 1000 things together randomly that the number is meaningless. It might as well be zero.

There are experts on DNA. They have known these numbers for a long time. They should be standing in awe of the intelligence that created this thing called "life."

Did the animal trainers of Darwin's day know that it was impossible to create new species? That would have stopped Darwin's theory in its tracks. But I don't think that physicalism was ever a scientific theory, right from the start. I used to call it "the physical hypothesis." But I think this was a credo, a belief system, right from the start, to get rid of the authoritarianism of established religion. I agree that it was a good thing to get rid of the authoritarianism of established religion, and that it advanced our culture, but now we are stuck with the authoritarianism of established science.

So I am asking the scientific establishment, and the whole academic establishment, if they would be scientific enough to consider Darwin's theory as a working hypothesis. I agree with the fact of evolution, and I recognize the "mountain of evidence" that supports it. I just don't agree with the WAY that Darwin said it happened. To avoid definition-switching, I don't use the word "evolution" to describe Darwin's theory. I call it "Darwin's theory of unintelligent design."

In 1870, people didn't make the distinction between the spiritual and religion. Even as late as 1951, when William F. Buckley, Jr. published *God and Man at Yale*, the issue was really established religion vs. physicalism. It wasn't until the Hippies came along, and discovered the spiritual independently of religion, that the culture became aware that the spiritual and religion were two different things.

So, in all fairness to the scientists of 1870, the Bible and the beliefs of traditional religion were not scientific evidence of a spiritual reality. The Judeo/Christian Bible could be taken as mythology, just as the Greeks and Romans had their mythology.

But since 1870, evidence of a spiritual reality has been creeping into our culture, from the British Society for Psychical Research, Mary Baker Eddy, William James, Edgar Cayce, Carl Jung, J.B. Rhine, Ian Stevenson, Richard Kieninger, and the Hippies. This is where the scientists have not behaved as scientists, but have acted like religious fanatics with a quasi-religious cult mentality. First of all, academic people who have taken a serious interest in the spiritual have been shunned and ostracized and have lost their whole academic existence. Second, scientists have adopted the infinite bias that any physical explanation is preferable to any spiritual explanation. Third, people who are able to dominate have asserted, "The spiritual does not exist; therefore all evidence of it has to be flawed." This last thing, by my logic, only proves that these people know absolutely nothing about the spiritual.

With these kinds of barricades in place, I don't see how establishment scientists are ever going to find any evidence of the spiritual. Their minds are closed.

ABANDONING THE STUDY OF THE MIND

The early psychologists were having problems studying the mind with something they called "introspection." The first problem was that they trained their observers in different methods of observation, so that their results couldn't be replicated by other scientists. Second, the subjects made errors in their observations. And third, some subjects lied about what they were observing.

John B. Watson came to the rescue in 1913 with his famous paper, "Psychology as the behaviorist views it," in which he suggested that psychology should become the study of physical behavior with the physical senses. In conclusion, he wrote,

> ... What we need to do is to start work upon psychology, making *behavior*, not *consciousness*, the objective point of our attack. Certainly there are enough problems in the control of behavior to keep us all working many lifetimes without ever allowing us time to think of consciousness *an sich*. ... ("Psychology as the behaviorist views it," 1913, pages 175-6)

This was entirely reasonable: "Let us see how much we can learn by studying human behavior." It did not invalidate the study of the mind using introspection, or even suggest that the study of the mind be stopped. But psychologists stopped studying the mind, following his direction, and started studying human behavior instead. By 1969, historian-of-science Duane P. Schultz wrote,

> ... No psychologist today calls himself a behaviorist – it is no longer necessary to do so. To the extent that American experimental psychology is today objective, empirical, reductionistic, and (to some degree) environmentalistic, the spirit, if not the letter, of Watsonian behaviorism lives on. ...
>
> (*A History of Modern Psychology*, 1969, page 236)

I have written long arguments in both *The Mental Environment* and *Dirty Science*, trying to figure out why the psychologists abandoned the study of the mind in favor of physical behavior. I think the main reason was because the physical scientists were enjoying such great success with the study of physical phenomena. And of course the belief known as "physicalism," or as Duane P. Schultz said, "reductionism," supported that and was supported by it.

I think that if the early psychologists had recognized that they were observing mental phenomena with mental senses and not vaguely "introspection," they would have had a better argument when the physical scientists accused them of not doing "science." Certainly, the early psychoanalysts, although not recognizing the mental senses per se, built an accurate body of knowledge using these senses, including discovering why people give false reports of their mental processes (psychological defenses).

The pretense of "objectivity" has been a major deception. I was not deceived by it. I described it in my 1970 manuscript. But the physical scientists have deceived themselves by it, in order to maintain their illusion that their perception of the reality was perfect.

The word "objective" refers to the object being perceived, and not to the subject doing the perceiving. There is no such thing as "objective perception" or "objective thinking." All perception and all thinking are subjective. Physical scientists try to hide that by speaking and writing in the impersonal mode, as in "It was observed" instead of "I have observed." But I am with Thoreau on that, when he said,

> We commonly do not remember that it is, after all, always the first person that is speaking.
>
> (*Walden*, page 3)

The insinuation, in calling their observations and their thinking "objective" is that there is no subjective factor operating here, and that therefore their observations and their thinking are 100% perfect.

The other error is that whatever happens in the mind is seen as "subjective" and therefore subject to error. Mental events, just like physical events, have an objective reality. It is just how either are viewed that is the subjective part. There is the reality and the perception of the reality. Physical scientists need to clearly differentiate between the two.

Physical scientists claim that observations of physical events with the physical senses are "objective" because they can be made by more than one person, whereas observations of mental events can be made only by one person.

Actually, observation by more than one independent observer reduces the subjective bias by the square root of the number of independent observers, but in no case does it reduce it to zero, as "objectivity" insinuates. Science is a collective subjective opinion, not "objective."

And scientists are not independent observers. They have all been indoctrinated into the in-group thinking of the social group "science" to which they belong. No amount of scientists are going to reduce this bias, because they all think the same way in this respect.

Actually, in most scientific studies, there are not multiple observers. Scientists studying gorillas don't all study the same gorilla. They each study their own gorilla, and then they compare notes. Their findings are scientifically verified by the process of replication.

In the same way, observations of mental events with the mental senses can be combined by replication with the observations of others to achieve something that can be called "scientific" knowledge.

Philosophers have argued that the mental senses are inaccurate, but so are the physical senses. We don't discard the means of perception that we have just because they are inaccurate. We find ways of checking their accuracy and correcting the inaccuracies.

"Objectivity" has been with us for a long time. It is entrenched. John Dewey advocated it in 1903. Rupert Sheldrake, in *The Science Delusion* in 2012, said that children in England were being taught to write in the passive voice, as in "The test tube was heated and carefully smelt" (pages 299-301).

It may take some gunpowder to break down the castle walls. I am saying that this claim of "objectivity" is fraudulent. Scientists making this claim should lose their credentials.

John B. Watson had no trouble abandoning the study of the mind. He simply asserted that there was no such thing as the mental. He asserted that what we call "thought" was nothing but sub-vocal talking. This is his complete argument:

> The behaviorist advances the view that *what the psychologists have hitherto called thought is in short nothing but talking to ourselves.* ...
> (*Behaviorism*, 1925, page 191)

And what kind of evidence does he present to show that all thinking is subvocal talking?

> ... The evidence for this view is admittedly largely theoretical ...
> (*Behaviorism*, 1925, page 191)

His assertions blocked my thought process for a while. I think he was one of those people with powerful mentalities who have hypnotic powers. I had to remember a difficult mental experience, how I explained to a friend how to know that the rungs of an extension ladder were locked in place, in order to break free of his force field. I didn't have the right words, and I was placing my hands in the same plane as each other to illustrate what I meant.

Watson right away is trying to deceive us by limiting the mental to "thought." Or maybe he was already deceived himself. The mental is much more than "thought." I remember a face. I feel emotions. I experience dreams. All these things are functions of the mental. And Watson never mentions the unconscious. (Actually, he uses the word "Voodooism" to smear "Psycho-Analysis" (*Behaviorism*, 1925, page 18).)

Then, by the use of the word "talking," he implies that all thinking is done with words. This is extremely annoying to me, because I make a huge effort to translate my thinking into words.

I remember a job interview I had, where I was explaining the Cost Allocation program I had written. The interviewer asked me, "How many overlays did it have?"

"What's an 'overlay?'" I asked.

When he explained to me what an "overlay" was, I told him the program had 7 overlays. It also had "user hooks" and a "meta-language," things I didn't know the words for. How could I have done these things if my thinking had to be only in words?

Watson's force field continues to influence the academic community:

1. We think only in words.

2. There is no such thing as creativity. It is all just a synthesis of known elements. (If we only think, and not create, and if we think only in words, then creativity has to be just a recombination or rearrangement of words.)

3. There is no such thing as intuition. (If we think only in words, then we don't think in pictures or patterns.)

4. Self-education is impossible — a delusion, a myth. (If we think only in words, and words of course come from the culture, then there is no thinking beyond or outside of or independently of the culture.)

I think some academic people need to examine the foundations of some of their beliefs.

Psychology has been steered away from the study of the mind, first to behaviorism, and more recently to the study of the physical brain, with the assertion, "The mind is nothing but the physical brain." But reincarnation research has shown some of us, anyway, that the mind continues to exist after the death of the physical brain.

Researchers in psychology are careful to study only physical phenomena with the physical senses. But then there is the hypocrisy that in order to know what is going on when certain areas of the brain light up, they have to ask their subjects what they are thinking, feeling, remembering, or dreaming. So the mental senses still play an important part in psychology, even though psychologists are not aware of them.

GETTING RID OF FREUD

In 1973, I read in *Harvard Magazine* that Freud was "out." A Harvard psychologist was quoted as saying he wasn't familiar with Freud. I couldn't believe it. That would have been disastrous to his professional reputation during the three quarters of a century that Freud was "in." It was convincing to me that Freud was really "out."

The rationale for rejecting Freud was that his discoveries weren't based on "empirical" evidence. By "empirical," they meant the evidence of the physical senses. They had no idea that there was such a thing as the mental senses and that Freud's discoveries were based soundly and solidly on the evidence of these mental senses. This evidence is just as "empirical" as physical evidence, and the discoveries made with it, as I have explained, are just as "scientific" as discoveries made with the physical senses.

Freud's star pupil, Carl Jung, was rejected immediately as a "mystic," when he observed that his patients were discovering the spiritual in their dreams. Freud would have been rejected immediately, too, if he had mentioned the spiritual. It is only because he didn't believe in the spiritual that his influence lasted as long as it did and his legacy is part of the cultural awareness of Western civilization.

But that legacy has to include the work of Carl Jung, even though he was rejected immediately and his discoveries are not as much a part of the cultural awareness as Freud's. He made many improvements to Freud's thinking and extended it into the spiritual.

So I see this legacy of both men as one body of knowledge, which I call "Freudian/Jungian depth psychology." It was backed up by the evidence of the mental senses. It was a whole new way of thinking, getting past the rationalizations and other defenses of the conscious mind into the ulterior motives that all normal people have. It was a way of thinking that I shared with my friends in New York in the early 1960s, most of whom were in therapy, too, recognizing subtleties of human mental activities well beyond conscious intellectualism.

And then this whole body of knowledge, this whole new way of thinking, was wiped out in 1973, by the consensus of an academic subculture that believed only in the physical.

I stand against this consensus of credentialed people in our accredited academic institutions. This was a wrong move, a bad move, a major step backwards for our culture, and a major step away from survival of the species.

My own theory is that this was a defensive reaction on the part of intellectuals. This new way of thinking made the intellectuals' way of thinking incomplete. It went beyond their thinking into levels of subtlety and depth and mental functions beyond their ken. They were not conscious of their real reasons for rejecting it, but found a rationale that looked legitimate and "scientific."

Of course also there were the smear tactics: "Freud did bad science." For lack of any supporting argument, that is only a smear.

And then there were Thomas Szasz, using more smear tactics, and Frederick Crews, who was brilliant enough to construct a persuasive argument, even though he had no experience with psychotherapy.

Then E.M. Thornton, in *The Freudian Fallacy: Freud and Cocaine*, was trying to invalidate Freud's discoveries and methods because he used cocaine. On the cover of the book is a really creepy distortion of Freud's face. Actually, as I have said, his use of cocaine may have helped him to break away from the Victorian culture of his time and formulate his radical new ideas.

I don't have to argue with any of these people. I have tested Freud's ideas and methods in my real life's experience. His basic ideas are sound, and his basic methods work.

In 2021, I bought *Freud: The Making of an Illusion*, by Frederick Crews, published in 2017. The word "illusion" makes it false. Even if this book is flawlessly written, that does not make Freudian psychology an "illusion." I experienced very real life-changing gains from Freudian/Jungian depth psychology. The book contains 666 pages of text, presenting Freud in a bad light. It is probably the longest rationalization ever written.

Crews, as an English professor, should know that an "ad hominem" argument is invalid. This is an "ad hominem" argument in the sense that presenting all the bad things and unscientific things that Freud did does not invalidate his basic ideas and methods, which have been tested by many people in real life and work.

A psychotherapist might point out that this man is extremely threatened by Freud and his ideas, and thus has this extreme defensive reaction, where he has to pour an enormous amount of time and energy into creating 666 pages of flawless text. A psycho-therapist also might point out that where Crews, as an English pro-fessor, knows that an "ad hominem" argument is invalid, he is sub-consciously creating this error as a cry for psychological help.

And what about his confession that he hadn't experienced psy-chotherapy? Why did he have to admit that?

I am wondering why this book was published by a major pub-lisher in 2017, many years after Freud was rejected in 1973. Of course Crews has published many books, and I'm sure that he is a favorite with the intellectuals and that he has a major platform. But going deeper than that, into Freudian psychology, I think the aca-demic people are insecure in their rejection of Freud and they need this book to reassure them that their decision was sound. Actually, in my opinion, it was probably the biggest mistake that was ever made in the history of our civilization.

BLOCKING THE ROAD TO SURVIVAL

This is as bad as it can be. This is catastrophic negligence. By ig-noring the spiritual, the mental, and Freudian/Jungian depth psy-chology, the academic establishment is actually moving away from my solution for the survival of the species. They are moving in a direction that is going to kill us all. And we can't argue with them, because they are trapped by severe sanctions against believing in anything beyond the physical.

No, the academic establishment is not actually taking us on a path to extinction. Hate and greed and our wonderful technology are doing that. It has often been said that our technology has raced ahead of our human ability to control it. We need to develop the human being to be able to use the technology responsibly. Freud and Jung gave us a way to do that. And the academic establishment is blocking that, allowing hate and greed to remain in control and take us down the rocky road to doom.

Ignoring things just makes people ignorant. And the academic establishment has attained this ignorance with methods that they all know are invalid and will not lead to accurate knowledge.

Smear tactics are more powerful than science. Calling some-body "bat-shit crazy" has more emotional effect than saying "p < .0001." But smear tactics won't get you the right answer. The right answer is what academic people want to get. They grade their students on having the right answer, not on how powerful their argument is. So how should they grade themselves?

Threatening to terminate a person's academic career is definitely more powerful than science. But it definitely does not give anybody the right answer. It destroys those basic principles of "academic freedom" and "freedom of inquiry" that are so essential to the pursuit of accurate knowledge. So how should the academic establishment grade themselves for accepting this social manipulation at the expense of accurate knowledge?

I would give them less than a failing grade. I would give them less than zero. More than just being ignorant, they are removing accurate knowledge from the culture.

Who am I to be giving the credentialed educators in our accredited academic institutions a poor grade? Again, the people with the status have the power. But it is not my status as an individual, but the truth of what I am saying, that counts. But I can't do this without important people to back me up. I have had confrontations with major corporations and persons of status in my computer career, and in all cases important people came to my side, because they could see that I was right. A few people have at least caught glimpses of the truth of what I am saying here, and more will follow.

A couple of reviewers of *Dirty Science* said that I was an expert who had studied the subject for many years and had done extensive research on it. No, I am far removed from academia, and I have done very little research. But the inaccurate opinions, attitudes, and beliefs in publications coming from academia are so obvious that anybody can spot them, except the people who have been indoctrinated into them.

Psychology is a mess. I sent out leaflets saying that to more than 600 psychology departments, around 2012, and did not receive a single response. But the move down, away from the study of the mental and Freudian/Jungian depth psychology, has really destroyed psychology. Psychologists need to recognize the mental senses and how they can be used, as they have been used in the past, to create a true science of the mind.

Instead, psychology has been dumbed down. We have this word "cognition," with the very broad meaning, "the mental action or process of acquiring knowledge and understanding through thought, experience, and the senses" (Internet, Oxford), whereas in the past those abilities have been differentiated as memory, reason, curiosity, perception, insight, intuition, creativity, and dreams. And what about will? Where does that fit in? And we have this word "consciousness," which isn't defined at all, except in the sense of awareness, and which needs to be differentiated further into mental senses and physical senses. And there is no mention of the "unconscious."

Going back to my college days, my decision to go into psychotherapy instead of getting a PhD in psychology was heavily influenced by a friend of mine, a psychology major, who told me, "People study psychology to find out what makes themselves tick. Really, they should be going to a psychiatrist." Psychologists' defenses would block them from finding out what makes themselves tick. Could it be that their defenses are blocking the knowledge of the whole field, too?

Psychology has studied in exhaustive detail the physical development of human beings, but it has not studied at all the mental development of human beings, namely their capacity for behavioral/philosophical development as they grow. Psychologists have not even formulated the concept of psychological age. One of the things that made psychotherapy so difficult for me was that I had to create knowledge that the professionals in the field had not yet created.

Academic philosophy has failed us, too. In *Dirty Science*, I faulted the academic philosophers for not thinking about the logical consequences of the arms race, especially when it became clear that it could lead to the extinction of our species. Somewhere I read that one of the functions of philosophy was "government." Where were they on that subject?

Socrates said, "Know thyself." This was important enough to be taught to me in my ninth-grade Ancient History, with no explanation of what it meant. So when Freud came along and gave us a method for self-knowledge, where were the academic philosophers? Didn't they see that this was an extension of Socrates's teaching?

I sent a leaflet out to 600+ philosophy departments around 2012, with the title, "Updating Philosophy." I said that academic philosophy hadn't yet made it into the 20th century (meaning

1900), because it ignored Freud's discoveries and methods. I received only one reply, saying, "Lots of luck!"

Academic philosophers in their pure thought might have asked the question, "What is wisdom?" They might have offered us some insights into how to live our lives. They might have offered academic people some insights into how to pursue accurate knowledge. I did take a course in Logic at Harvard given by Willard Van Orman Quine. That's about as far as they got.

Sociology, too, has failed us. Sociologists never got much farther than the gang on the street corner. They never recognized, as I did, that the same social laws govern all social groups. They never acquired the self-knowledge of seeing how these social laws applied to their own academic departments and the whole academic subculture. Harvard and Yale may be rivals on the football field, but they conform to the same norms of this academic social group.

Sociology has also failed to show us how binding these social laws are. I read a whole sociology textbook. It told me of the wonderful diversity of human cultures. It never mentioned how people were bound to their culture by threats of ostracism or death. Going against your country is "treason," and you are a "traitor." You can be executed for this. An American woman was arrested recently for joining ISIS. Going against your religion is "blasphemy" or "heresy." People used to suffer horrible tortures and horrible deaths for even being suspected of such a thing. Now, we have freedom of religion in the United States, but in less-developed nations, these punishments are still going on.

I have always felt that academic people believe they are superior – that the laws that apply to ordinary people don't apply to themselves. They certainly see psychotherapy as something for inferior people. And maybe the reason why sociologists haven't gone beyond the gang on the street corner is because they fear, on some semi-conscious level, that those same social laws might apply to themselves. And why don't academic philosophers work on self-knowledge? Because, of course, self-knowledge is the key thing they are avoiding.

What all academic people need is some self-knowledge of the social group they are in, how irrational are some of its beliefs, especially the belief in a purely physical reality, and how binding these beliefs are.

I don't know how that is going to be accomplished. I do believe that the vast majority of academic people are sincere scientists and scholars, who don't go along with the irrational beliefs, but stay silent to protect themselves from social ostracism. Some of them are going to have to come forward.

How many men died in the Normandy invasion? Nobody is going to die here, but they may lose their academic careers – temporarily. But then they will be hailed as heroes, when the vast majority take over. Then the ones who dominated before will be identified as the villains.

This reminds me of the Bob Dylan song, "The Times They Are A-Changin'." The times need to change if our species is going to survive. The American academic mind needs to wake up from its hypnotic trance.

CHAPTER 5

What Is Philosophy?

American academic philosophers call themselves "professional philosophers." They are truly "professional" because they earn a living teaching it. I can't call them "so-called 'professional'" philosophers. But are they truly "philosophers?" Are they truly doing "philosophy?"

They limit themselves to "pure thought." They don't even deal with evidence. That would make them "scientists," they say. Dealing with practical problems, such as the threat of nuclear annihilation, is beneath them. Methods of improving the mind to be better able to do "pure thought," methods such as Freudian/Jungian depth psychology, meditation, and yoga, are not part of "philosophy" as they define it. All they really have is logic, and that logic is not always accurate.

It seems that they are limiting themselves to what the ancient Greeks were aware of – conscious reasoning processes. They haven't yet made it into the 20th century (yes, I mean 1900), to recognize that there are unconscious forces making those conscious reasoning processes inaccurate.

They are still asking the question, as the ancient Greeks did, "Of what can we be certain?" They haven't yet made it into the 1700s, to discover probability theory, where nothing is treated as certain.

The ancient Greeks saw reason as the highest mental ability. This is still true, as reason makes the final decision, based on input from reason, memory, curiosity, perception, intuition, insight, creativity, unconscious forces, will, and dreams. It seems that contemporary philosophers see reason as not only the highest mental ability, but as the only mental ability.

Memory + reason = intellect. Intellectualism limits itself to those two functions of mind. And intellectualism dominates the "pure thought" which is American academic philosophy today.

If that is what they want to do, then they certainly have a right to do it. But they are leaving a huge area of potential knowledge untouched.

The word "philosophy," when it is used as "the philosophy of" anything, is the thought behind that thing, whether it be science or marketing or baseball, or whatever. And the word "philosophy" without the "of" is understood to mean "philosophy of life," or the thought behind the living of life.

These professional so-called "philosophers" have appropriated the word "philosophy" to mean their very narrow subset of what can legitimately be called "philosophy." But they have the credentials, they have the position, they have the status, and they have the power to define this word "philosophy" any way they want to. However academic people want to define a word, that is what the word means.

So now we have this wide, wide area that I have described as "an activity with no name." I came up with a name for it, "software for living." But why should I have to invent a new name for it, when this is truly "philosophy," in its oldest and widest sense? The academic people were wrong in appropriating the word "philosophy" to mean some narrow slice of it. Again, they are the academic people. They are the consensus of the credentialed experts in our accredited academic institutions. They tell us what is "right" and "wrong." You don't tell them they are wrong.

So I have to reach for deeper truths. What is "philosophy," really?

Western academic philosophy started with Socrates. He defined "philosophy" with a question: "How should we live?"

In asking "How should we live?" he is reflecting the authoritarianism of the teacher. He is trying to tell everybody how to live. I define "philosophy" with the personal question, "How shall I live?" Because we are all unique, the best way to live would be different for each of us. To define it in a more definitive way, I define "philosophy" as "the application of the mind to the living of life."

The word "philosophy" comes from the Greek words "*philo*" and "*sophia*," meaning "love of wisdom." It doesn't say it means doing anything about wisdom. It only says it is the love of wisdom, as in sitting around adoring it. But at least we know that it has something to do with wisdom. And what is wisdom?

Wisdom is far more than just the conscious intellect. First of all, you have to have knowledge. And to have knowledge, you need to have evidence. You need to have tested things and verified them in your real life's experience. That requires perception, both with the physical senses and with the mental senses. The high end of wisdom also requires psychic abilities, to read other people's thoughts, to sense their medical conditions, and to see the future, among other things. This is achieved by reaching psychological age 28, according to Richard Kieninger.

The whole idea of psychological age brings up the whole new idea of psychological development that the ancient Greeks never heard of. In fact, our present culture has only seen it in the writings of Richard Kieninger, because *Re-Educating Myself* is not yet part of the cultural awareness. First of all, the whole idea of psychotherapy was unknown to the ancient Greeks. The whole idea of unconscious forces influencing our lives was unknown to the ancient Greeks. And then, it seemed to me, from reading Freud, that he saw the unconscious as a fixed place in the mind. My actual experience, in going through psychotherapy and dream analysis, was that I was bringing what was previously unconscious into consciousness. I dreamed that what was once underwater became a beautiful land of trees and flowers. I can see, if one were to go farther than I went, that one's consciousness might open more and lead to clairvoyance.

And then there were the mental attributes that I didn't think I had – creativity, intuition, and will – that were brought up out of my unconscious in psychotherapy. All of these things play a part in wisdom. Just being able to use one's whole mind as opposed to being limited to one's conscious intellect gives a person a much greater potential for wisdom.

Psychological development is a major component of wisdom. What my dreams taught me was wisdom. Appropriate behavior, which is the goal of psychological development, is wisdom – to do exactly what is necessary in any situation, in order to achieve the desired result.

The ability to differentiate, which comes from psychological development, is a very important part of wisdom. One must know the difference.

Socrates said, "Know thyself." That should make self-knowledge a part of what philosophy is. It was 2400 years before Freud came along and showed us how to do that. Freudian/Jungian depth psychology is an extension of Socrates's teaching and should be included in philosophy – not the practicing of it, which is psychology, but undergoing it, as part of one's education.

Undergoing psychotherapy, as I have already said, leads to wisdom in many ways. Also self-knowledge is knowledge, which is one of the components of wisdom.

So we have all these components of wisdom:

– the use of the whole mind, not just the conscious intellect
– knowledge, including self-knowledge
– psychological development, to develop appropriate behavior and bring unconscious factors into consciousness
– the ability to differentiate, fine-tuned as "discernment"
– fine-tuning the perceptions to include psychic abilities

If "philosophy" is the "love of wisdom," then philosophy is the love of all this, whether or not it does anything about it.

The web pages of philosophy departments that I have seen also use the expression "the good life" as one of the goals of philosophy. Intellectual debate will not take you to "the good life," but the attributes I have listed will, especially psychological development.

To me, the first ingredient of "the good life" is a good sex life. Has philosophy ever dealt with human sexuality? This is a very powerful drive, more powerful than any vows taken to suppress it. It is something that needs to be dealt with consciously and positively. Religion teaches us that sex is sin. We learn about sex from other eighth graders, who don't know any more about sex than we do. All we have is our psychological defenses against this powerful force which threatens to overwhelm us and ruin our lives. So the word "fuck" becomes the dirtiest swear-word, and "It sucks" and "up yours" become negative statements instead of the positive sexual pleasures that they represent. Instead of having psychological defenses against this powerful force, we need to accept this force into our lives and make it an important part of "the good life." For that, we need teachers in the eighth grade, not just to teach us the biology of sex, but also to teach us how to deal with it philosophically.

All these things are legitimately part of "philosophy," from Socrates saying "Know thyself" to the "love of wisdom" and "the good life." Our professional philosophers in our accredited academic institutions have arbitrarily limited themselves to a small sliver of that, which they call "pure thought."

Even the pure thought has problems. I have noticed, in the few books I have read on philosophy, that the logic isn't always accurate. Philosophy needs to be written in a computer language (yet to be invented), so that the logic can be checked by a computer.

Also the abstract words used in philosophy aren't always defined clearly, and not all people have the same definition. Abstract words need to be uniformly defined by a subroutine or function in this same yet-to-be-defined computer language, so that all people are using the same definition of the word.

Right now, what the academic people are doing that they call "philosophy" is really useless. I can't stop them from doing what they are doing. But I can call upon the rest of you to ignore what these academic people are doing and apply this name "philosophy" to this "activity with no name" that I have been doing, which has everything to do with the application of the mind to the living of life.

We all have a life to live, we all have a mind to tell us how to live it, and we all do philosophy, whether we are aware of it or not. So the first rule of philosophy should be that it should be comprehensible to people with average intelligence and even below-average intelligence. I have been surprised in my life by the intelligence shown by people who were considered "mentally retarded," or "mentally challenged" as is considered politically correct nowadays. Most human beings have a certain basic intelligence to make intelligent decisions in their lives.

The language of philosophy needs to be a simple language that can be understood by the greatest number of people – "life," "love," "truth," "knowledge," "wisdom," "falsehood," "good," "evil," "work," "play," "experience." Christ knew more than any person here on earth, and yet he expressed his teachings in simple parables.

I learned, when I went straight from Harvard into Basic Training in the Army, where most of my buddies had not been to college, that I could have intelligent conversations with them if I just didn't use the big words I had learned in college. This was reinforced in psychotherapy, where my psychiatrist insisted that I use a specific, factual language, as opposed to abstract language. The way to get at the truth is to focus on the facts, not abstract theories, which are fiction.

How shall I live?

Actually, very few people ever do philosophy, because by the time we are old enough to think about it, we have already been totally programmed. Otto Begus was forced to do philosophy because he was in the Hitler Youth as a child, and then of course had to change his whole way of thinking. I was forced to do philosophy because I was faced with the prospect of nuclear annihilation if our culture continued in its ways of thinking.

Without those kinds of incentives, we are all programmed into the in-group thinking of all the social groups we have belonged to. The first group is your parents, teaching you their opinions, attitudes, and beliefs. Then you pick up the thinking of your parents' social class (rich, middle, poor, upper middle white collar, lower middle blue collar), ethnic group, social group, political party, nationality, and religion. You immediately learn when you go to school that if you want the other kids to like you, you must adopt the attitudes, behavior, and dress of the peer group. And what they didn't teach us at Harvard, when they gave us freedom to think, was that it was freedom to think their way. They didn't know that they were bound to dogma just as rigid as the dogma of the Catholic Church, and more insidious because it was not written, not spoken, not defined in conscious terms, and not coming from any known authority.

So when we are ready to begin thinking consciously about how we want to live our lives, we have already been indoctrinated into the thinking of a great many social groups. It is too late for any "pure thought." We have already been programmed.

So the choice, before we can do "pure thought," is to decide that we want to endure all those horrible things that people can do to us, such as loss of approval, loss of social status, loss of love, loss of income, and loss of life. Also, we have to rid ourselves of all the in-group thinking that has already been programmed into us. I don't think that is possible without psychotherapy.

These social pressures create a bias that must be overcome if we are to use our own minds to determine how we live our lives. The answer to "How shall I live?" is that you will live, behave, and think as your social groups dictate you will live, dress, behave, and think.

The reason why people think and believe so differently is because their various social groups force this upon them.

So I hope you will be motivated by the threat of nuclear annihilation, as I was, to break free of the in-group thinking of your social groups and do some philosophy. The threat is still there, 66 years after the novel *On the Beach*, as China parades its nuclear missiles that it can fire at us undetectably over the South Pole, and Putin is rattling his 1600 nuclear weapons. Really, if we have survived for this long, it is only because God is protecting us from ourselves.

Chapter 6

My Philosophy

Yes, I was innocent when I wrote *Re-Educating Myself*, but that innocence did not in any way diminish the accuracy of my philosophy. It only gave me a false view of how my philosophy might be received by the culture.

The idea itself of "cultural awareness" is not part of the cultural awareness. Scholars know that Carl Jung described the self-steering process in a 1931 paper, and that Aristotle said that the way to happiness is to develop one's potential as a human being, and that Locke and Kant were aware of the mental senses, before they were confabulated into something called "introspection" by Western academic philosophers. But it is not what scholars know, in their exclusive circles, but what is part of the cultural awareness, that moves the culture at large. That is why I am still trying to sell a million copies of *Re-Educating Myself*.

Not much of my philosophy has changed since I wrote *Re-Educating Myself*. Actually, it is presented there in much more detail, and with much more intelligence, that I am able to do at age 89. This is more a summary of things I have already said, many times over, with emphasis on those things which are not part of the cultural awareness.

We come into this world knowing absolutely nothing. At least the physical brain knows nothing, and before we are able to speak, most of us have forgotten everything we have known in past incarnations.

We are immediately programmed with information from the culture by our parents and teachers and actually anybody who is older than we are. We are ready to believe them, from the time we were small children and our parents were as gods to us. But all of this is only "information," and not "knowledge," until we have tested it in our own experience and found it to be true. Most of it is true, and most of it can be tested immediately based on things we already know to be true, but some of it is not true, or cannot be tested immediately.

In our childhood upbringing, we are supposed to believe persons of status on their "authority." When we are adults, we are supposed to believe persons who are experts in their fields as "authorities." I put "authorities" in quotes, to mean "so-called 'authorities.'" We don't know that these people are telling us the truth unless we know as much as they do. The way we know that an expert is telling us the truth is to check with another expert or get references from satisfied customers.

I have a book on Indian philosophy which tells me what "the seers" know. I'm sure the seers are pretty much right about what they are saying, but this is not "knowledge" for me until I have tested it in my own life's experience and found it to be true.

The real authority, not in quotes, that we all have, is the authority to decide for ourselves what to believe. That doesn't make it true, but at least we are on the right track.

As we come of age, as we finish the childhood force-feeding, as we get ready to accept adult responsibilities, it is time to switch over from our childhood submission to "authorities," to recognize one's true authority to decide what to believe and how to live one's life. We may not be the most knowledgeable or the most intelligent, but it is our authority as adults.

As adults, we are told that we are supposed to be "responsible." But we can't have responsibility without authority. The first step in taking responsibility is recognizing that we have the authority.

I begin my philosophy by saying, "I don't know." The cornerstone of my philosophy is the solid rock of ignorance. I don't pretend to know what I don't know. That way, I actually know more than those "authorities" that pretend to know but really don't know. I know that I don't know.

The beginning of wisdom is the confession of ignorance. This was totally against the in-group norms when I was at Harvard. Nobody was allowed to admit ignorance. But how can you learn anything unless you are willing to admit you are ignorant?

Most philosophies start out with a fixed framework, like a picture frame, which is taken to be absolute truth: "God created the heavens and the earth and all living creatures in 6 days." "There is no reality beyond the physical or what can be explained by known physical laws." Whichever picture frame we choose, we can fill in our picture from there.

I know nothing about absolute truth. Everything I know is relative truth.

There is a real universe, which is the collection of everything that exists. There is also a subjective universe, which is my perception or representation of that real universe. That perception of the real universe does not start at some ultimate boundaries. It starts at my perceptual center, at what I call my "I-center," and it builds a sphere of knowledge out from there. This knowledge is only relative truth, not absolute truth. As I acquire knowledge, this sphere gets larger.

I have two tests to determine what I put in my sphere of knowledge. The first is "internal consistency." Is it consistent with everything else I know? If yes, then add it. If no, there is an error somewhere. There are no contradictions, inconsistencies, or paradoxes in the real universe. Whatever exists cannot cause another thing that exists to not exist. Therefore there can be no contradictions, inconsistencies, or paradoxes in my subjective universe, if it is to be accurate. Any inconsistency has to be an error in my thinking.

The other test is "dynamic consistency." As new knowledge comes in, is it consistent with everything else I know? If it is not consistent, then is the new knowledge false, or is something in my sphere of knowledge false? I spent hours and hours and hours after psychotherapy sessions, as new insights came in, with my mind churning away, trying to resolve it all.

I asked myself in the beginning if I could use logic. By "logic," I mean one's ability to reason and the man-made systems of logic and mathematics that have been built upon that. I didn't know at the time that people would come along and tell us to reject logic. But when they came, I was ready for them. I can't live a life on earth without using logic. I can't put on my clothes in the morning, or find food, or find my way home at night, without using logic. I can't have knowledge without logic, because I wouldn't know what is true or false. And it is always worth repeating that without logic, we would all die in head-on collisions immediately.

Logic will tell me what is false, but it won't tell me what is true, except within the logical system itself. In order to have any knowledge of the reality beyond that, and even to be aware of the logical system itself, I need something else. I need perceptions.

How do I know anything about the real universe? The only way I know anything is through my perceptions, my senses.

Philosophers have pointed out, first of all, that our senses don't sense the ultimate reality, that they don't sense the sub-atomic particles or waves or whatever substance is beneath that. This is true. So we just have to function with the senses that we have. If we were a creature with only one antenna to sense the world, we would have to make do with that.

And the holy man tells us that all is illusion. But if all is illusion, then why doesn't he fall through into nether space? Or if all is illusion, then he is illusion.

My senses tell me relative truth about the reality I am functioning in. I know that all is not illusion because real things are happening to me every day and I am functioning relative to these real things. I sense that my elbow is hard, and that the table-top is hard, and that if I bang my elbow on the table-top, it will be hard. All I need to know is that I am functioning relative to this reality I am functioning in, whether or not it is all ultimately an illusion.

Philosophers have argued that the senses aren't reliable. We see mirages. Some people are color-blind. Some people are blind. Again, that is no reason to reject the senses. We just have to live with the senses that we have.

So if we think we might be seeing a mirage, we just have to get closer to it to see if it is water, or feel it, or taste it. Traffic lights in the United States are designed with the red on top, for the benefit of people that are color-blind. By combining the various senses with the reasoning power of the mind, we get around the unreliability of the senses. In computer technology, people have learned how to create reliable systems out of unreliable components. This is seen as a fairly new idea. But people have been doing it with their perceptions all along.

And then along comes quantum mechanics, which has shown that reality is altered by our perception of it. But those changes are observable only at a sub-microscopic level. The gross appearance and behavior of the reality doesn't change. The temperature of a bucket of water changes when a thermometer is stuck in it, but this change is not perceptible to the human senses.

If the only way we know anything about the reality is through our senses, some smart person is going to come along and say that maybe we don't just perceive the reality. Maybe we create in our minds the thing that we perceive.

Somebody has already done that – George Berkeley, in the 1700s. He asserted that whatever exists only exists because somebody has perceived it.

This has created enormous problems in philosophy. Phenomenology goes through enormous convolutions to describe people's perceptions without assuming that the things they are perceiving actually exist. We need to prove George Berkeley's theory wrong or go through the convolutions of phenomenology.

I have read that Samuel Johnson disproved George Berkeley's theory, but all I can find on the Internet is that Samuel Johnson kicked rocks.

There is a reality independent of our perception of it. When you stub your toe on something in the middle of the night, you didn't create that something by stubbing your toe on it. It was a pre-existing thing that you didn't know about.

Every child learns, by the age of two, that when their mother has left the room, she hasn't ceased to exist. But that argument can be dismissed as an illusion that all children share.

I think George Berkeley's idea has become part of the cultural consciousness as a hypnotic implant. It is obviously absurd, but I never found a way to disprove it, until this year 2023.

When I lived on a dirt road in New Hampshire, I was the person who heard the tree fall in the forest. Here were these millions of trees that nobody had seen. Berkeley would have argued that God had seen them. But that is getting away from the argument. If God exists, then God is aware of everything. The argument is that human beings create the reality by their perception of it.

And it can be argued that airplanes have flown over that wilderness and thus created the trees by people's perception of them. But what about the many life-forms beneath the trees, life-forms that nobody has seen? Do they come into existence the instant that somebody perceives them?

No, they don't. There is a growth process that all life-forms of a given species have to go through to reach their present state. That growth process can be studied for members of that species. Therefore it can be assumed that the life-form newly discovered has come into existence as a result of that growth process and not as a result of having been newly discovered.

And so I assume that George Berkeley's theory is false. There is a reality independent of our perception of it.

I take this as proved, along with the proof of reincarnation. These are basic assumptions of my philosophy, which I accept as "knowledge." I think it is necessary to announce that these are basic assumptions of my philosophy. There is always the possibility that they might be proved wrong, but meanwhile I am moving ahead, accepting these assumptions as "truth."

I put my arms in a circle above my head, to represent my little sphere of knowledge. There is always a little opening at the top of the circle, to indicate that I am always open to new knowledge. But if you are trying to tell me something that "the seers" know, it may be true, but it is probably beyond my little sphere of relative knowledge, so I have to treat it as only a working hypothesis.

This is science – being open to new knowledge, formulating working hypotheses, and testing for internal consistency and dynamic consistency. The professional philosophers are wrong when they exclude scientific methods from "philosophy." Applying scientific methods to the living of life is both "science" and "philosophy." The Brotherhoods call themselves "scientist/philosophers."

And as part of my little sphere of relative knowledge, I accept everything that has been proved by science. Scientists don't even use the word "proved," because things aren't proved absolutely in science as they are in mathematics. But they can be proved "beyond a reasonable doubt," as is close enough for our legal system, and that is close enough for me. 2500 cases suggestive of reincarnation is good enough for me, to prove that the mind is more than just the physical brain. And I didn't even need Daryl Bem's figure of about one chance in 75 billion that people were "Feeling the Future" purely by chance. I had already had perceptions of the future in my own life's experience.

This does not mean that I accept all the authoritarian pronouncements that scientists make. I accept only what has been proved beyond a reasonable doubt, in my opinion, by legitimate scientific methods.

The ancient Greeks asked, "Of what can we be certain?" The only things I am certain of are the man-made systems of logic and mathematics. I approach everything else as a gambler. Probability theory, something the ancient Greeks didn't have, is an important part of my philosophy. I ask myself, "What are the odds?" In most cases the odds aren't mathematically defined, so I have to separate my knowledge into gradations of "possible truth," "probable truth," and "almost certain truth. Nothing, except for the man-made systems of mathematics and logic, is absolutely certain. It might all be an illusion. The world might end tomorrow.

Socrates said, "Know thyself." I say, "Love thyself." It is a key ingredient to "the good life" and especially to sexual pleasures. You have to believe you deserve such pleasures.

New Age gurus have told us that we have to get rid of the ego. I am saying, with the backing of Carl Jung, that the way to love of oneself and "the good life" is to strengthen the ego. But first we have to define what we mean by "ego." The "ego" is the sense of self, the real self. We have to identify that real self and bring him or her to maturity.

The way I developed my real self was through psychotherapy and dream analysis. I have told that story before, so I won't repeat it.

Psychotherapy represents a whole new way of thinking. It opens up aspects of the mind that the intellectuals don't even think exist. The intellectuals know just enough about psychotherapy to know that it makes their way of thinking incomplete, and so their psychological defenses have rejected it. Any freshman class in "critical thinking" can see that their arguments against it are invalid.

The most important thing to know about is the thing that does all the knowing – the mind. Psychology has abandoned the study of the mind for the study of physical phenomena observable with the physical senses. Psychology has also rejected the legacy of Freud and Jung, which was making some progress in the study of the mind, because it wasn't based on "empirical" evidence, meaning the evidence of the physical senses.

But empirical evidence can also be evidence of the mental senses, those senses that all normal people have, to observe our thoughts, our emotions, our memories, and our dreams. The body of knowledge that Freud and Jung assembled was based on the evidence of these mental senses. I think that the psychologists would have had a better argument, when the physical scientists accused them of not doing "science," if they had known that their knowledge was based on the evidence of the mental senses. Psychologists today, when a section of the brain lights up, still have to use the evidence of the mental senses. They have to ask their subjects what they were thinking, feeling, remembering, or dreaming, in order to know what was really going on in their minds.

Observations with the mental senses are limited to observation of one's own mind, unless one is clairvoyant. If scientists want to observe other people's minds directly, they will have to become clairvoyant. This can be achieved by psychological development to the maximum, according to Richard Kieninger. Meanwhile, they will have to rely on hearsay. But psychotherapists can identify when that hearsay is inaccurate. They can spot psychological defenses, because arguments that appear accurate to a person who really wants to believe them are obviously invalid to the therapist.

The Hippies rejected the mental in favor of the spiritual. They even demonized the mental, calling it a source of error. While it is true that the mind can be a source of error, the way out of that is not to reject the mind. The mind is still there, making its errors, although not consciously. This is just driving a person deeper into errors. The way out of it is to make a conscious effort to identify the errors and correct them. This is accomplished through psychotherapy.

I have been an explorer of the mental, exploring my own mind and developing it psychologically. It seems that I am the only person studying the mental, so that should make me the foremost expert on the subject. But then there is nobody in a position of authority to report my findings to.

But you, the reader, are in a real position of authority to decide what to believe. You can replicate my findings, if you choose. A similar person following a similar procedure should experience similar results.

And what is the similar procedure?

I didn't become a new human being through psychotherapy alone. My psychiatrist did his job by bringing me up to normal. I resolved my traumatic experience and changed my "human nature" in dream analysis. But psychotherapy gave me the necessary disciplines to enable me to interpret my dreams successfully.

What are the disciplines I learned in psychotherapy?

I think the most important was learning to see my psychological defenses and get around them. I learned that the longer I argued, the more likely it was that it was a rationalization. Also if I was defending myself emotionally and vehemently, it was likely to be a psychological defense.

Also essential to psychotherapy was finding my real self and becoming that real self, instead of playing some role as an actor.

You can find your real self by just reflecting back on the time when you liked yourself the best. If that time is not the present, that is important information that you can take to the therapist.

Learning how to interpret my dreams was also essential, so that I could continue my therapy with dream analysis.

Trying to see where I was at fault in every situation was an important attitude that I brought with me into therapy.

Becoming an observer of my physical actions and my thoughts was also an important discipline. My psychiatrist asked me to tell him everything I did and everything I thought, from the time I woke up in the morning. He put me through that drill for a long time. I was being trained to be a scientific observer of myself.

Uncovering mental abilities I didn't know I had – creativity, will, and intuition – was important because it enabled me to use a greater part of my mental potential in resolving my psychological problems and interpreting my dreams. Intuition, especially, or "playing my hunches," was particularly important in interpreting my dreams.

Dreams are a natural part of what we are as human beings. Freud recognized that they were giving us valuable information about who we were. Jung improved on that. I got a valuable education from my dreams. When I paid attention to them, they showed me the greatest wisdom I have ever seen.

Dreams do not tell you the truth. They speak in symbols and riddles that you have to figure out for yourself. Therefore they are not like the authoritarian education you had as a child. They are more appropriate for an adult, recognizing that you have the authority to decide for yourself what to believe.

Your interpretations of your dreams don't all have to be correct. Like a teacher correcting your homework, the dreams themselves will correct you, or present the message in a simpler way. This "self-steering process," as I have called it, was known to 4 out of 6 people at my table at the 2013 dream conference. But I have not seen it in popular published books. I don't think it has yet become part of the cultural awareness. In fact, I think the culture is actually moving away from recognizing dreams as important sources of information.

But the fact that dreams are able to correct you implies that the dreams are coming from some source that knows the truth.

And what is this source that knows the truth? Do dreams come from God, as the man in the Hawaiian shirt was suggesting to me? Dreams could very well come from higher beings. We know that the television programs don't come from within the TV set, so why assume that dreams are coming from an unconscious part of our own minds?

Richard Kieninger has warned that dreams can also come from lower entities that want to influence us in negative ways. I experienced this once in a dream about my sister June, when suddenly I realized that it was another entity faking the appearance of June. It hasn't happened to me very often. It is just something to watch out for.

So where do dreams come from? I really don't know. They might come from God, or they might come from higher beings and occasionally from lower beings, or they might come from one's own unconscious mind. All I know is that they are a source of truth, not in an authoritarian way, but in a way that is compatible with one's own authority to decide what to believe.

Do higher spiritual beings exist? I am not a total believer on that. Yes, the awareness, acceptance, and assimilation of the spiritual were absolutely necessary for me to reach the compassion and altruism necessary for my "human nature" itself to be changed. But the "spiritual" could have been just symbolic, representing my highest values and ideals. The same with my death experience, shooting up into the presence of the Light and of Christ. They could have just been dream symbols, as compensation for my depressed state of mind at the time.

I see no way that life on earth was created by random combination of chemicals according to known physical laws. Even the simplest living entity is much too complex for that. The only way that I can explain how living creatures came into being is that they were designed by a higher intelligence.

And animal breeders have known, probably right from the beginning, that Darwin's theory was wrong. They have never been able to create a new species, even with human intelligence. Creating a new species by random mutation would be even less likely. Natural law prevents that, with those individuals at or near the norm being more robust than those at the fringes, which are more likely to be sterile. So the forces of nature would keep the members of the species at or near the norm. Somebody had to be doing genetic engineering.

The presence of life-forms on earth is the strongest argument I know for the existence of higher beings.

I have seen the power of prayer. My prayers to Christ for protection enabled me to bubble up effortlessly from spooky dreams. I don't even have spooky dreams any more. The prayers were that powerful.

At a meeting of the Psychic Experiences Group (PEG) at The Rhine Research Center, I said that I was beginning to believe in the power of prayer, and they all laughed at me, not because they thought I was deluded, but because I even had a doubt. They were all absolutely certain of the power of prayer.

I am a math person. Writing has been an agonizing chore for me in the past. But recently I have been praying to the angels to help me with my writing, and words and phraseology and whole sentences have come to me effortlessly. This whole chapter is about 99% a first draft. (No, this is not automatic writing. These are my own ideas. It is only that the right words to represent those ideas have come to me more quickly and easily than before.)

So I would say that the preponderance of the evidence favors the existence of a spiritual reality and the existence of higher beings within that spiritual reality. Whether it is proved beyond a reasonable doubt, I don't know. Why I even have a reasonable doubt, I don't know.

I guess it is like atomic and sub-atomic physics, where physicists don't actually see the entities they are working with. Other people, such as Edgar Cayce, have had perceptions with which to view the spiritual, but I haven't. I am limited by the perceptions I have. No, I have never seen an angel, but I don't have to believe on faith. Like the physicists with sub-atomic entities, I believe on the basis of logical inference.

I am asking you to accept the existence of a spiritual reality only as a working hypothesis, as with anything else I am saying.

And for members of the scientific community, it is absolutely required that you accept the existence of a spiritual reality as a working hypothesis, until such time as it is proved or disproved scientifically beyond a reasonable doubt. That would be the scientific approach. Holding the fixed belief that the spiritual does not exist is not within the scientific way of thinking and should cause you to lose your credentials as a scientist.

We don't live in a free country. We are all bound by the "social laws" of the social groups we belong to. We must conform to their norms and at least pay lip service to their opinions, attitudes, and beliefs (OABs), or face ridicule or expulsion from the group. We are bound by the tyranny of the people we call our "friends." That is why people think and believe so differently.

I have incorporated into my belief system, as working hypotheses, the teachings of Edgar Cayce and Richard Kieninger. Obviously Edgar Cayce was wrong about the "earth changes" he prophesied for the end of the 20th century, and Richard Kieninger was wrong about Armageddon and Doomsday, which were also supposed to occur at that time. But there is still a wealth of information in the legacies of both men.

I should also mention the many teachings that I have NOT incorporated into my belief system. We have had L. Ron Hubbard, Timothy Leary, Baba (Saint) Ram Dass, the Hippies, the Maharishi, the Reverend Sun Moon, Krishnamurti, *In Search of the Miraculous*, Werner Erhard, Carlos Castaneda, *The Aquarian Conspiracy*, Seth, and *A Course in Miracles*.

Some of these are the "false prophets" that the Bible talked about. Basically they have influenced the culture in a negative way, towards confusion. But there are bits and pieces of valuable information coming from them, such as the invention of the e-meter in Scientology. If that were used as a biofeedback device instead of as an interrogation device, it would be a valuable tool in psychotherapy. And from *In Search of the Miraculous*, I learned how some people suck energy out of you.

I have discovered that the academic community is dominated by a belief in a purely physical reality. This belief has not been determined scientifically, but is supported by unscientific arguments, which all academic people know are unscientific, in the name of "science." This is fraudulent.

I have coined the expression "mental warfare" (and "mental combat" and "mental bullying") to mean those invalid and destructive methods used by academic people from their positions of power, to put other people down. If lawyers use illegal methods, they are disbarred. Similarly, if academic people use methods that are illegitimate, they should lose their academic credentials.

MY VISION OF GOVERNMENT

A majority of people who have reached the psychological age of puberty in the United States will elect public officials who are motivated the same way they are, by compassion and altruism. Government will be seen, not as having power over people, but as a service organization, to maintain an infrastructure and to protect the people from those that would do them harm, both from within the country and from outside of it. We would have to maintain the best possible weapons technology, including nuclear weapons, as long as the other major nations did not go along with us.

First of all, in order for a majority of people to reach the psychological age of puberty, the culture would have to adopt the concept of psychological age, and then we would have to find ways to measure it. My suggestion is that tests of the ability to differentiate would be a good indicator of psychological maturity. Tests of compassion and altruism would indicate whether a person had reached the psychological age of puberty, which I will just call the "key age."

Tests of psychological maturity can be developed with longitudinal studies of children, identifying when they switch over from the childish answer to the mature answer, and also identifying those whose psychological growth has been arrested. While these tests are being developed, we can use the tests of psychological wellness that we already have.

Everybody needs to go to a psychotherapist, just for an evaluation of their psychological condition. Nobody is qualified to make this determination for themselves, not even psychologists. After the necessary psychological testing, the people who have reached the key psychological age will be given a written statement confirming that from their psychotherapist. This written statement will be a legal document, like a birth certificate.

Adults who have not reached the key psychological age will be encouraged to undergo psychotherapy. Government funding needs to be available for those who can't afford it. Funding for this could also come from private charities.

Children whose psychological growth has been arrested will have psychotherapy as part of their school curriculum.

People would only have to go to therapists for long enough to acquire the necessary disciplines to interpret their own dreams. From then on, they could continue their psychological growth on their own with dream analysis.

Lucid dreaming, or being aware that you are dreaming, is not important. I always used it to pursue a sexual fantasy. The important thing about a dream education is that you are not in control. The dreams will teach you things you never knew and answer questions you never thought to ask.

When I went to Harvard, everybody had to be able to swim, in order to get a Harvard degree. I think it would be more appropriate to require that everybody reach the key psychological age, in order to get a college degree.

So, when tests of psychological age have proved to be reliable and have become established, it should be required that a person reach the key age in order to get a college degree, run for political office, become a police officer, or vote. The voting requirement might be attainable only when a majority of people have reached the key age, but I think that the people who are true adults will be respected by those who are not, so that it could happen even with a minority of adults at the key age or beyond.

That step will quickly transform our culture in America, but how would we persuade the other major nations to go along with us?

First of all, they would be as children, psychologically, and we would be as adults. They would have the same respect for us that all children have for adults that are truly psychologically mature. They will recognize our authority as adults and respond to it.

My cousin who married a Japanese woman and stayed there after the war said that the Japanese had a very high regard for us because we defeated them in warfare (instead of wanting revenge, as one might expect). If people who have been our enemies to the death can become our friends, then certainly it is possible that people who have been hostile to us can respect us when they see that we are truly being adults.

But if anybody is seriously challenging us, being psychologically mature will enable us to stay ahead of them in weapons technology.

I am hoping that people in other nations, and leaders of other nations, will follow our example because they respect us.

I think if we could get a majority in each of the major nations of the world to come together on this, then we would be able to establish a world government. Again, this would not be a government to have power over people, but a service organization, to protect people from harm.

Right now, I would say that those major nations are the ones that have the nuclear weapons – the United States, Russia, China, India, Pakistan, Great Britain, and France. I would say that the job of all these nations right now is to see that no other nations have nuclear weapons. If Iraq or North Korea are developing nuclear weapons, a United Nations police force should go in there and stop them.

The United Nations has the power to do this. But the United Nations does not have the power to stop Putin's war against Ukraine, because Russia is one of the three nations that have veto power in the U.N. That is the failure of the U.N.

We need a new system for world government. We need all the major nations to sit down at a peace table and subordinate themselves to the will of all humanity for the protection of all humanity. This can only be accomplished if those leaders are psychologically mature.

This is extending "do no harm to others" to all humanity, but only in respect to international warfare. Warfare between governments will be banned, but all other government functions will be handled by the individual governments.

The first step in "do no harm to others" would be for the major nations to get rid of all weapons of mass destruction and require all other nations to do the same. The world government would have the power and the authority to go into any nation and forcibly remove such weapons. Also, as people work on their psychological development, a few are likely to become clairvoyant. These people would be able to detect whether there was a secret lab somewhere developing germ warfare – or whatever.

But that is all pie in the sky. First we need to recognize, and deal with, the forces of evil (FOE).

CHAPTER 7

Forces of Evil (FOE)

I am putting this chapter last in hopes that you will read the rest of this book before throwing it in the trash. It seems that any use of the word "evil" is grounds for immediate disqualification in any rational discussion. The forces of evil (FOE) assure that. As the Jesuit priest said in the movie, *Bless the Child*:

> The Devil's greatest achievement is that people don't believe he exists.

I am not talking about traditional views of "Satan" or "the Devil." I am talking about the Black Mentalists, as described by the Brotherhoods to Richard Kieninger. These are not fallen angels, but human spirits whose karma is so bad that they cannot incarnate, or if they did, they would suffer a horrible death immediately. Because they are doomed, Richard said, they want to drag down all the rest of us with them. So they communicate to us via telepathic suggestion, trying to influence our lives in a destructive way.

The first two people I told about the Black Mentalists called me "paranoid." But they were not professional psychologists, and they had not done the necessary psychological testing to determine that I was paranoid. So what did they mean by calling me "paranoid?"

I see it as a defensive reaction. It is a scary thing to think that there are evil entities out there in utter darkness that want to put destructive thoughts into your head, so that they can drag you down with them. I lived in fear of the Black Mentalists for 9 months after I first read about them.

151

So why haven't they dragged us down with them already? Because they are like the bullies in the schoolyard. They are not more powerful than all human beings. Human Masters and Adepts are more powerful than they are, according to Richard. He gives the example from the Bible of when the pharaoh's priests flung down their staffs, which became snakes, and then Moses flung down his staff, which became a snake and gobbled up their snakes. This was all done by hypnotic delusion. Moses's power to implant thoughts hypnotically was greater than that of the priests.

According to the cosmology described by Richard, there is a whole hierarchy of higher beings – God, the celestial host, archangels, angels, and human Masters and Adepts. That whole hierarchy of higher beings is called the Holy Spirit. Any one of those beings is more powerful than any Black Mentalist. As long as we don't get on the wavelength of the Black Mentalists with such things as hate, greed, or an unethical pursuit of power, or actively contact them, as with a ouija board, we are protected. And if there is any doubt, the Protective Prayer, "Dear Christ, Please protect me," will call upon those higher beings to protect us.

I use the Protective Prayer constantly, whenever I suspect evil influences are trying to get into my life. I use it in traffic when somebody is getting too close or is driving in some strange way. I use it on an airplane when a little voice keeps suggesting that the plane could crash, that it could explode at any minute as the plane did over Lockerbie, Scotland.

You have to believe, or at least have the working hypothesis, that higher beings exist, and that these higher beings will protect you, in order to deal with the fear of Black Mentalists. Denying the existence of Black Mentalists won't help you. It is a well known psychological defense. What you don't know, or refuse to know, CAN hurt you. Your best defense is to recognize its existence and then learn to deal with it.

What I am trying to do here is to get around the psychological defenses. I can't discuss this subject rationally if I am up against psychological defenses.

And to start the rational discussion, I am asking you to accept the idea of Black Mentalists only as a working hypothesis, to be verified (or not) by you in your own life's experience.

And then I want to point out the things that I see as evidence of Black Mentalists and their influence.

Reincarnation research has shown that human beings do not cease to exist when they die. Their physical bodies die, but there is at least a mental component that keeps on going.

Hitler and Saddam Hussein and all the evil people that have ever existed have not ceased to exist when they died. Their mental component is out there somewhere, unless they have already reincarnated. And, as they have tried to impose their will upon us here on earth by the most violent methods, it is reasonable to assume that they would want to do the same when they were discarnate entities.

I have read a couple of books by British authors that said that Hitler collaborated with demonic forces in his quest for world conquest – that they gave him his brilliant ideas and charisma, and then dropped him, to let Germany be reduced to rubble. I present this only as a working hypothesis. I was interested in researching this but realized that that would not be possible because I don't know German.

To start with, psychological defenses could be coming from Black Mentalists. The knee-jerk reaction of "paranoid" did not come from psychological testing. So where did it come from? If psychological defenses were hypnotic suggestions, that would explain why they are so binding and so difficult to get around.

Let's look at the black tuxedos of the wealthy, the black suits of men in the highest positions of power, and the black robes of the clergy. First of all, people living in New York are excused. When I lived there, black was the most practical color to wear, because of the amount of soot in the city.

We all know that politics is corrupt – that many people get into political office through lies, deceptions, and character-assassinations. Politics could well be influenced by Black Mentalists.

But what about rich people? Did rich people get their money dishonestly? I am sure that many rich people earn their money honestly, but also many rich people have more money than they have rightfully earned by their contribution to humanity. Richard Kieninger talks about "financial karma." People can incur karmic debt by getting more money than they have earned. And did Black Mentalists help them to do this? I leave this as an open question. It needs to be considered on a case-by-case basis. It is all part of the working hypothesis.

The clergy, of course, is holy. It is sacred. But just this quality of being beyond criticism can lead to corruption.

In recent years, priests have been found guilty of sexually molesting children. Is this the influence of Black Mentalists? I think this has happened because the Catholic Church has demanded sexual abstinence of its workers. The Church has not recognized the power of human sexuality – it must find an outlet somewhere.

I think if the Black Mentalists do influence organized religion, it is much more subtle than that. We may need to reach a higher level of psychological maturity just to recognize it. Certainly, the corruption of the Catholic Church led to the various Protestant religions, and the authoritarianism of the Protestant religions was a major factor in the scientific rejection of religion and the spiritual. Certainly, this authoritarianism, this demand of unquestioning obedience to beliefs that human beings are not absolutely sure of, can be called "corruption." But I would rather skip over that and go right to the authoritarianism of the belief system that dominates our culture today – physicalism.

All academic people know that threatening to terminate, and actually terminating, a person's academic career, because of subjects they might be interested in (levitation, voodoo, spirit entities), are invalid arguments.

All academic people should know that accepting any physical explanation over any spiritual explanation creates an infinite bias against the spiritual.

All academic people know that the assertion, "The spiritual does not exist; therefore the evidence for it must be flawed," is an invalid statement. It has not been proved, and cannot be proved, that the spiritual does not exist.

So why are academic people so rigidly bound to the belief that the spiritual does not exist? In *Dirty Science*, I called this "mass hypnosis." And what causes hypnosis? Something called "suggestion." And how do Black Mentalists communicate? By something called "telepathic suggestion." So I advance the hypothesis that Black Mentalists are putting this belief in a purely physical reality in the heads, and keeping it in the heads, of a dominant minority of the academic community, to blind them to the truth of things that they should know.

I support my hypothesis by citing all the invalid arguments that are used to support the assertion that the spiritual does not exist.

In *Dirty Science*, I picked apart Richard Dawkins, James Randi, James Alcock, and Ray Hyman, showing all the smear tactics they were using. I showed how the National Academy of Sciences, people whose scientific credentials are literally "awesome," were duped into making a statement that is "forever recorded in the annals of folly." I described how Wagenmakers et al. tried to refute Daryl Bem's paper on "Feeling the Future" by changing the math. I said:

> In other words, in Bayesian analysis, they are able to plug their bias into the equation, and out the other end comes an answer that reflects their bias. What's wrong with that?
> (*Dirty Science*, page 162)

First of all, all of these people are attuned to the forces of evil by using invalid arguments. But the main thing is that they all start out with the premise, "The spiritual does not exist." That is the absolute conviction that they build on. That sounds like a hypnotic suggestion to me.

All those people who call themselves "skeptics" but really have a belief in a purely physical reality that can't be changed, first of all are being false by calling themselves "skeptics." If they were truly skeptics, they would also be skeptical of their belief in a purely physical reality. Being false puts them in tune with the forces of evil, but, more important than this, their absolute conviction in a purely physical reality is an indication that a hypnotic suggestion may be implanted in their heads.

These so-called "skeptics" will just smile at you while you are arguing the existence of a spiritual reality, absolutely certain of their belief. But please do not be mesmerized by their certainty and their ridicule. These are just weapons of mental warfare.

There are no Black Mentalists on earth. People on earth are only influenced by Black Mentalists. I have read that this influence can be detected by the black in people's auras. This is a way to detect the influence of Black Mentalists scientifically.

I see 3 causes of psychological problems – physical, mental, and spiritual.

Physically, a person's brain may not be working properly. This is now recognized and treated with drugs.

Mentally, a person's brain is working properly but has been overwhelmed by one or more traumatic experiences. This is treated with the traditional talk therapy.

And spiritually, yes, some people are possessed by demons. But we should not despise them for that. We should love them and try to rescue them.

The movie *The Exorcist* was based on a true story of a boy, age 14, who was possessed by a demon. The priest, in order to save the boy, let the demon come into his own body.

Wikipedia calls this "hearsay." To Wikipedia, it is hearsay, because they weren't there. But to the boy and the priest, who were there, it was very real.

Most of us are not totally possessed, as this boy was, but all of us, except for Masters and Adepts, are influenced to some degree, I believe, by the telepathic suggestions of Black Mentalists. So if we demonize people who are possessed by demons, we are demonizing ourselves.

Jungian analysts in Great Britain recognize this spirit interference and treat it.

I have seen the color black working its way into the culture in many ways. The African Americans wanted to be called "black" instead of "negro" or "colored." In 2011, I had a hard time finding a guitar strap that wasn't either black or had skulls on it. What does this say about popular music? In the past year, I have noticed many athletic teams wearing black, in addition to their traditional colors. I just saw the Boston Celtics wearing so much black that I could hardly see the green.

There never used to be mass-shootings by depraved individuals. Now they are happening more frequently all the time. And what about suicide-bombers? Are these people being influenced by the forces of evil?

But most serious of all, our culture is being steered away from survival by a rigid belief system that could be a result of mass hypnosis by these forces of evil.

Are we at least allowed to ask the question?

Quiz

This is a "true" and "false" quiz of the material in this book. A statement is "true" if it accurately represents the viewpoint of the author in this book, whether or not it is actually true.

You can record your answers as the number of the question, followed by "t" or "f," as in "1t2f3t..." and email to happinessandsurvival@gmail.com. You will get a grade in reply.

1. All normal people have mental senses to perceive their thoughts, emotions, memories, and dreams.

2. "Psychological age" refers to one's level of psychological development.

3. The normal adult in our culture is psychologically 10 years old.

4. At the psychological age of puberty, "human nature" itself changes, from exclusive self-interest to compassion and altruism.

5. If your interpretation of a dream is wrong, the dreams themselves will correct you.

6. In order to evolve spiritually, you must get rid of the ego.

7. We are all interconnected.

8. The mind is nothing but the physical brain.

9. Reincarnation research has shown that the mind exists independently of the physical brain.

10. When we are young children, our parents are as gods to us, all-powerful and all-knowing.

11. Freud did not back up his theories with empirical evidence.

12. Carl Jung was a mystic.

13. Edgar Cayce was playing a well-known con game.

14. Gurdjieff and Krishnamurti were major influences in this philosophy.

15. You are the highest authority to decide for yourself what to believe.

16. There are forces of evil in the spiritual realm.

17. People who believe in the spiritual are uninformed, unintelligent, superstitious, and/or delusional.

18. Psychotherapy can save us from nuclear annihilation.

19. The collective psychological defenses of an entire culture got rid of Freud.

20. The people best qualified to read this book are people who have had some successful psychotherapy.